W R Lethaby   1857–1931   Architecture, Design and Education

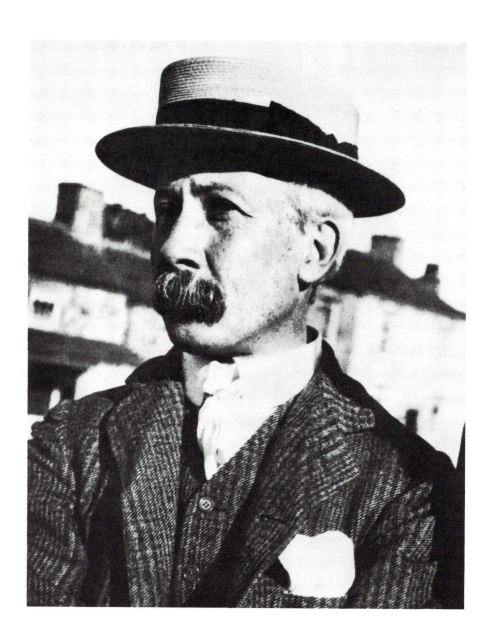

Edited by Sylvia Backemeyer and Theresa Gronberg

W R Lethaby
1857 - 1931
Architecture, Design and Education

Lund Humphries London

Copyright © 1984 Lund Humphries Publishers Ltd

First edition 1984
Published by
Lund Humphries Publishers Ltd
26 Litchfield Street London WC2H 9NJ

ISBN 0 85331 485 3

Designed by Herbert Spencer
Typeset in Imprint
(which was invented at the Central School)
by Tradespools Ltd, Frome
Made and printed in Great Britain
by Camelot Press, Southampton

This publication is a companion volume
to the exhibition of the same name
held at the Central School of Arts and Crafts, London
from 22 October–17 November 1984
and subsequently
at the Cheltenham Art Gallery & Museum
from 22 December–2 February 1985

Contents

Lenders

The Art-Workers' Guild
Visitors of the Ashmolean Museum, Oxford
Major N.Biddulph
Rev. J.Bradberry
John Brandon-Jones
British Architectural Library, RIBA
The British Museum
M.J.H.Bunney
Central School of Art & Design,
Library & Archives
Peter Cormack
Anthony C.Davies
John Dreyfuss
Dean & Chapter of Gloucester Cathedral
Leicestershire Museums,
Art Galleries & Records Services
William J.Nelson
North Devon Athenaeum, Barnstaple
North Devon District Council, Barnstaple
Margaret Parsons
Hon. Sara Peel
Canon G.R.S.Ritson
Royal Academy of Arts
Dr Godfrey Rubens
Society for the Protection of Ancient
Buildings
Tate Gallery
Victoria & Albert Museum
A.B.Waters
Dean & Chapter of Westminster
Mr and Mrs Christopher T.Whall
William Morris Gallery,
London Borough of Walthamstow

Sponsors

The Exhibition committee gratefully acknowledge the generous financial support of the following organisations and individuals:

Gordon Baldwin
Barclays Bank
Colin Cheetham Designs
David Crisp (Crisp & Wilson)
Design Council
Simon Enthoven (Enthoven & Mock)
Eva Reckitt Trust
Noel Fleury (Bissell Appliances)
Guild of St George
John Gunter
ILEA
Dick Linklater
A.G.Lisle (Chapman/Lisle Associates)
Ian Logan Design Co.
Bill Newland
Olivetti
Raymond Loewy International Ltd
Derek Roberts
Martyn Rowlands
Royal Society of Arts
Douglas Scott
David Stubbs
Weaveplan (E.Ellis)
Robert Weaver
John Weeks (Llewelyn-Davies Weeks)

Foreword

This exhibition is a unique and long-overdue tribute to our first Principal, W.R.Lethaby – the forceful disciple of Pugin, Ruskin and William Morris. We aim to present Lethaby in his many roles of architect, lover of craftsmanship, designer and educationalist. His ideas were not always immediately accepted in this country, but ironically, as in our own times, this was not so abroad. Particularly in Germany, his many writings and methods influenced the development of functionalism at the Bauhaus and as a consequence much of what we now accept as the 'norm' in the education of artists, craftworkers and designers. Lethaby was a founder of the Central School of Arts and Crafts and we have therefore felt it appropriate to limit the exhibition to the period ending in 1911 when he left the School to devote himself full-time to the Professorship of Ornament and Design at the Royal College of Art.

There was an earlier exhibition here in 1957 to mark the centenary of Lethaby's birth and to accompany the unveiling of the blue plaque on the Southampton Row façade of the School. The present exhibition is much more ambitious and will offer the opportunity to re-examine his fundamental philosophy and achievement by all who visit the exhibition or have access to this catalogue. Lethaby was undoubtedly a man of both intellect and practical ability, whose contribution to our own time is appreciated by too few; this exhibition seeks to provide material evidence that will afford him the honour he deserves.

I would wish to offer my thanks to the Lethaby Exhibition committee comprising Sylvia Backemeyer, Tag Gronberg, David Reeves and Peter Matthews who was its chairman; to Godfrey Rubens for his knowledge and enthusiasm, to John Laing, John Myers and Andrew Watson for photography, to Christopher Cook for publicity and to Helen Atkinson for the poster which has been both designed and printed in the Central School. The background research was supported by Michael Kennedy, Godfrey Rubens, Peter Cormack and our own Library staff. The catalogue, the permanent record of this event, was in the hands of the joint editors and exhibition selectors, Sylvia Backemeyer and Tag Gronberg. I am, of course, equally grateful to all those, too numerous to mention here, who kindly agreed to lend us exhibits; their names are listed in the catalogue as are those of our sponsors, whose generosity has enabled us to meet the cost of this show.

My gratitude is also due to Ken Mellor, of the GLC Architects' Department, for designing the exhibition and to all those members of staff who gave support during the preparation period.

Finally, Lund Humphries Publishers Ltd have published this catalogue and especially warm thanks are due to John Taylor and Herbert Spencer for their very helpful collaboration in its production.

Tom Pannell
Principal
Central School of Art and Design

Introduction

William Richard Lethaby started life while the memory of the Great Exhibition was still fresh and died within a year of the March on Rome by Mussolini's Fascists. In youth, he saw that last and grandest monument to the Gothic Revival, G.E.Street's Law Courts, rising in the Strand and in age, the building of Walter Gropius's Bauhaus at Dessau. After a brilliant but conventional career in which he made a considerable reputation as a sensitive designer in several traditional styles, he became almost overnight an outspoken apostle of plainness. He was, indeed, one of the first architects in Europe to propose an architectural revival established on the principles of sound building construction, materials, economy of structure and fitness for purpose and not on the invention of another style. As a basis for criteria of design he eschewed taste and aesthetic experience and, in 1896, the year in which the Central School of Arts and Crafts was opened, spoke of the need to sweep away all theories of art design, proportion, picturesqueness and pretty drawing styles, and to identify architecture with reasonable building. Design, he said, was only making up one's mind how a given work should be done under certain circumstances; the ingrained idea that there were certain art shapes that could be combined to make an art design was so much cant.

Lethaby saw architecture as the matrix of civilisation – thus all building, however humble, and all cities, however squalid, and the life therein were the exact expression of contemporary society. Although his ideas and proposals for reform were neither so eloquently nor so trenchantly expressed as those of William Morris, they were sincere nevertheless and sprang from the same moral and Socialist critique. Some of them have become the commonplace of design and architectural theory and teaching, but others, concerning the relationship of art to life, await for their fulfilment some far more fundamental social change.

Lethaby's influence on architectural thought in this country was greater than any other of his own time and greater in fact that most of his contemporaries realised, but it was expressed through his teaching and more widely through what he wrote rather than through his architecture. Until comparatively recently his few remarkable buildings were little known; one of the first to draw attention to their importance was Nikolaus Pevsner, who described Lethaby's church at Brockhampton as one of the most convincing and impressive for its date in any country.

This exhibition of Lethaby's work as an architect, designer and teacher, though it cannot, of course, recapture the charisma of the man – taking place as it does in a building largely designed by his students – will facilitate a new evaluation of his designs and serve to demonstrate his wide pedagogic influence. It was not, said many of his students, that Lethaby ever showed you how to do things. He just showed you how to think about them.

Godfrey Rubens

Chronology

1857   Born 18 January in Grosvenor Street, Barnstaple, Devon

1860   Family moves to Ebberley Lawn, Barnstaple

1869   Student in the Department of Science and Art Drawing Class at the Barnstaple Literary and Scientific Institute

1871   Apprenticed to Alexander Lauder the architect

1876   First drawings published in *The Building News*

1877   First prize of £5 in *The Building News* Designing Club, using pseudonym 'Debut'

1878   Moved to Duffield, Derby to work for Richard Waite

1879   Worked for T.H.Baker in Leicester for three months
Awarded Soane Medallion
Moved to 21 New North Road, London
Started to work for Norman Shaw as Chief Clerk

1880   Moved to 20 Calthorpe Street
Admitted as Student at the Royal Academy
First Soane journey in Northern France
Awarded Pugin Travelling Studentship

1881   Royal Academy Tite Memorial Prize
Pugin Tour in West Country

1882   £15 Prize in Goldsmiths' Hall Silverware Competition
Second Soane tour in Loire Valley

1883   St George's Art Society founded
Exhibits at Royal Academy
£35 Goldsmith's Hall Silverware Competition

1884   Art-Workers' Guild founded
Exhibits at Royal Academy

1885   Exhibits at Royal Academy

1888	Arts and Crafts Exhibition Society founded – First Exhibition. Exhibits 2 drawings
1889	Arts and Crafts Exhibition Society – Second Exhibition. Exhibits a number of works First public lectures. Sets up in practice at 9 Hart Street (now Bloomsbury Way)
1890	Kenton & Co. founded
1891	Moves to 2 Gray's Inn Square, London WC1 Kenton & Co. exhibition Joins Society for the Protection of Ancient Buildings
1893	Elected to the committee of SPAB Visits Constantinople
1894	Appointed Art Inspector to the Technical Education Board, London
1896	The Central School of Arts and Crafts opened Lethaby and George Frampton appointed joint directors of the Central School Herman Muthesius arrives in England William Morris dies
1901	Appointed Professor of Ornament and Design, Royal College of Art Moves to 15 Duke Street, London W1 Marries Edith Rutgers Crosby
1902	Lethaby appointed Principal of the Central School
1903	Buys 111 Inverness Terrace, London W2
1906	Appointed Surveyor of Westminster Abbey
1907	Deutsche Werkbund founded
1908	New Central School building opened
1911	Resigns from the Central School Elected Master of The Art-Workers' Guild
1915	Philip Webb dies Design for Industry Association (DIA) founded
1918	Resigns from LCC and RCA Moves to Hartley Wintney, Hants
1920	Appointed Surveyor of Rochester Cathedral, Kent Returns to 111 Inverness Terrace
1922	Art-Workers' Guild presentation on 65th birthday

1922	Awarded Hon.D.Litt.Manchester University
	Modern Architecture Constructive Group founded
1924	Refuses RIBA Medal
1926	Made a Freeman of City of Barnstaple
1927	Edith Lethaby dies
	Resigns surveyorships of Westminster Abbey and Rochester Cathedral
1931	Dies on 17 July

Lethaby and his wife seem to have made at least one visit to the Continent in most years between 1900–1914

Lethaby as a young man
(see catalogue entry 11d)

William Richard Lethaby
and the Central School of Arts and Crafts

by Theresa Gronberg

'Probably the best organised contemporary art school', was Muthesius's verdict on his visit to Lethaby's Central School of Arts and Crafts.[1] In the years following its foundation in 1896, visitors from abroad appeared regularly to assess this new British experiment in art education. But as one enters the imposing, purpose-built Edwardian building in Southampton Row, it is difficult to conjure up the pioneering and improvised atmosphere of the early Central School of Arts and Crafts, first temporarily housed in Regent Street. The Central School which opened its door to students in the autumn of 1896 was in many ways a very different establishment from the one we know today. And yet Lethaby's ambitions and aims in establishing the School, and as its first Principal, remain remarkably relevant almost ninety years later. Then as now, the question of the day was the relationship of education to industry. Lethaby proposed schools of art which would function as

> 'training classes for the expert designers who should be so much in demand for all our industries. Our foreign competitors, who in attacking our commercial position have had the proverbial advantage of the offensive, have taken our ideas in art as in other things, have experimented with them, changed them a little and then frequently undersold us in our markets. They have experimented unceasingly, and have employed design experts just as they employed experts in chemistry and mechanics'.[2]

Too few students, Lethaby felt, were being employed, or indeed attracted, by British industry.

Attempts had been made throughout the nineteenth century to harness art education more effectively to industry. But Government-initiated reforms, such as William Dyce's Schools of Design and, subsequently, the art schools controlled by the Department of Science and Art under Henry Cole, suffered from an over-bureaucratic administration and were to have little impact on contemporary design. The dismal standard of British manufacture at the Great Exhibition of 1851 had aroused official disapproval; but it was the more progressive critics who saw that the real solution lay in linking a revival of handicrafts to an aesthetic based on the idea of fitness to purpose. John Ruskin and William Morris both vehemently rejected the DSA schools' training of art teachers, a system which involved copying from historical ornament, progressing painstakingly from the delineation first of plane, then of solid geometrical forms. Such a mechanical approach, they felt, stifled creativity, and in their view, it was workers, not prospective teachers, who were most in need of training and education. After the report of the Royal Commission of 1886, which provided yet further evidence that Britain was lagging behind other countries in industrial technology, various attempts were made to improve technical education. The Technical Instruction Act of 1889 granted county councils the power to levy one penny rates towards technical education for the artisan classes; and the 'Whisky Money', a tax levied on spirits in 1890, was in part used to finance technical education. But these were half-hearted and ineffectual efforts.

Ultimately, it was at the level of local government that the most exciting developments ensued. In 1892 the London County Council established a Technical Education Board with instructions to provide 'as its first duty, considerable further facilities for practical and technical education in the poorer and manufacturing districts of London'.[3] Sidney Webb, the Fabian chairman of the Board, set up a special committee and commissioned an investigation into technical education in London. The result was Hubert Llewellyn Smith's *Report on Technical Education* (1892) which, after reviewing many types of institution, concluded that everywhere the teaching in design and modelling was deficient. One of his recommendations was that the TEB administer grants to art schools on the condition that design, modelling and at least one manufacturing process be taught. He provided a list of twenty-one crafts he felt might be offered, suggested that the schools be subject to regular inspection and concluded with the hope that 'some day the Council may be able to establish a great Municipal Art School of its own'.[4] The Board reacted promptly to the Report, and circulated an advertisement for the post of art inspector. The future inspector was to act as adviser to the Board on all matters relating to art teaching. Among the 166 applicants was the architect and designer William Richard Lethaby, who submitted glowing references from Richard Norman Shaw, William Morris, Burne-Jones, Walter Crane and Philip Webb. Lethaby was duly appointed joint part-time Inspector along with George Frampton, a sculptor and fellow member of the Art-Workers' Guild. Both intended to continue their work as practising artists. The Board went on to establish a school of its own in 1895, the Bolt Court Technical School specialising in lithographic processes. It was independent of the Department of Science and Art, and all the teachers were specialist printers. Results from this school were favourably assessed by Lethaby and Emery Walker and compared well with standards abroad. Acting on suggestions proposed by the Inspectors, Sidney Webb formally proposed that

> 'the Board should extend its very successful experiment at Bolt Court, and set up in some central situation an art school of its own . . . such a school would enable the Board to provide specialised art teaching in its application to particular industries'.[5]

This was to be the Central School of Arts and Crafts.

The first premises of the Central School of Arts and Crafts were rented and consisted of two buildings – Morley Hall, formerly occupied by the Young Women's Christian Association, at 316 Regent Street, and a house at the back facing Little Portland Street. Lethaby agreed to allow his name to be put forward for Principal; three applicants were interviewed, but no appointment was made, and it was decided to make Lethaby and Frampton part-time Directors. Harry Bates ARA and John S. Sargent ARA were to act as Visitors. Although Frampton was nominally co-Director, accounts of the period reveal that he was rarely present, and Lethaby was therefore given free rein to implement his ideas – and his choice of staff. As at Bolt Court, all the instructors were to be craft practioners, and Lethaby dispensed with the notion of paper qualifications and Art Teachers' Certificates. The *Technical Education Gazette* published the aims of the Central:

> 'It provides for apprentices, pupils and workmen engaged in, or connected with, artistic handicrafts the best instruction in art and design as applied to their particular industries. No attempt will be made to meet the requirements of the amateur, or to do the work of the teacher of figure and landscape drawing and painting; nor is the instruction given directed in any way towards the preparation of pupils for examination. The special business of the school will be the industrial application of decorative design, and students will be expected to concentrate their studies on the several branches of the industries in which they are engaged'.[6]

The new type of teaching pioneered here, with its emphasis on crafts and the lack of examinations, and the part-time instruction by specialists, marked a significant break with the DSA art schools. The October 1896 issue of *Punch* exulted over the opening of the Central in doggerel:

'Charge, Frampton, Charge! On Lethaby on!
. . .
British workmen don't lead where so long they have led;
The foreigner's filching our honour and hoard.
Let us hope that our national wooden-head
May be cured by the Technical Board!'[7]

But the new school, because it resembled no other art institution, aroused bewilderment as well as excitement: some time after its opening, a prospective student in dairy farming was misdirected to the admissions office in Regent Street.

As both staff and students were employed in the daytime, all classes were held in the evenings, but workshops were at the disposal of students during the day. Fees were carefully calculated so as not to exclude suitable candidates: apprentices, 'learners and improvers', were admitted free. An eyewitness account of 1897 gives a vivid impression of a typical student's interview:

'The next applicant . . . is a sturdy fellow of about 13, who has done some drawing at the Board School, is just apprenticed to a cabinet maker, and wants to learn furniture design. He brings his master's certificate of apprenticeship in his hand, is promptly accepted, and sent down to begin work at once in Mr Christie's designing class.'[8]

From the first admission of about one hundred students in 1896 numbers soared, proving that there was a growing demand from professional workers to expand the vocational education they received as apprentices.

This emphasis on education through the direct handling of tools in a workshop environment was central to Lethaby's philosophy. To him, an abstract and theoretical approach to art was like trying to learn to swim in a thousand lessons, but without water. He urged prospective students to specialise in a particular handicraft but, at the same time, felt it was essential for a worker to perceive the links between his own and other crafts: 'you must go upstairs and see how stained glass windows are made and books are bound and gilding done'.[9] Although an accomplished scholar, Lethaby was personally unassuming, and all his teaching was directed at demystification. Here he acknowledged a debt to William Morris; in a lecture delivered at the Central School, Lethaby recalled how in his 'young and aesthetic days' he was puzzled when William Morris had said how much he valued cooking. At the time, Lethaby thought it a vulgar remark, but had come to see that unless one cared for cooking as an art one could not care for anything else.[10] Lethaby thus evolved his famous definition of art as being a well-made thing: 'art is not a special sauce applied to ordinary cooking; it is the cooking itself if it is good. Most simply and generally art may be thought of as the *well doing of what needs doing*.'[11] Similarly, 'design – that mysterious word! – is only disposing elements in proper ways and arranging how work shall be done'.[12] Teaching should therefore foster a proper understanding of tools, materials and function and the notion of art as service rather than as expression of genius.

Lethaby's approach to the teaching of drawing and design, not surprisingly, bore no resemblance to the methods employed by the schools of the Department of Science and Art. Everyone should, Lethaby felt, draw just in the way everyone was expected to learn to write. Drawing he regarded not so much as a skill but as a means of seeing, recording and thinking and he advocated that all advanced drawing should be carried on in association with the student's particular craft. Like Ruskin, who had advocated a minute and reverent study of nature in his classes at the Working Men's College, Lethaby encouraged designs derived from natural forms. For example, Catterson-Smith's Thursday evening classes at the Central School consisted of a lecture on certain underlying principles of design followed by a nature study, which was then adapted to the requirements of the students' individual crafts.[13] This workroom was also well supplied with casts, sculpture and colour reproductions. Most of the classes had access to historical and technical examples of their craft for purposes of study and drawing, and in addition, there was a lively display in the School's entrance hall of Japanese prints, pottery, metal work and reproductions. Lethaby placed great value on studying the history of the arts and crafts, but he disapproved of the mindless copying of second-rate casts which formed so large a part of the DSA curriculum. It is perhaps difficult for today's student to appreciate the vital rôle once played by 'examples' in art education. In a period when slides were not widely available for teaching, and foreign travel inaccessible to artisans, school examples in the form of casts and reproductions were in huge demand. But students at the Central were fortunate in being able to draw on two sources: the Central School's own collection and the Schools Examples Collection housed within the School, which functioned as a kind of circulating library for art schools.

It was Lethaby who was largely responsible for choosing the items for the Schools Examples Collection, and he was required to report regularly on his purchases. His shopping list makes fascinating reading: numerous portfolios of art facsimiles, specimens of metal work and textiles, collections of photographs, textbooks on heraldry, drawings, botanical books and magazines, and, of course, the obligatory plaster casts. The Central School's own collection was even more varied: Douglas Cockerell presented several loose sheets of Kelmscott Press work; Selwyn Image, who had loaned Christopher Whall some cases of butterflies for a lecture at the Central, offered to donate the entire collection. In 1901 Lethaby was authorised to purchase some large cartoons for stained glass by Burne-Jones. Professional firms often made gifts to the School, such as E. and U.Richardson of Elswick Leather Works, Newcastle, who sent a set of skins and samples illustrating the whole process of leather preparation. A study of historical examples was crucial, Lethaby felt, to modern design because

> 'usually the best method of designing has been to improve on an existing model by bettering it a point at a time; a perfect table or chair or book has to be very well bred'.[14]

This attitude may seem fairly remote from modern ideas of individual inspiration and expression. But Lethaby was certainly not advocating an unimaginative or timid repetition of earlier forms: to study the past in order to achieve understanding was his aim.

Lethaby took an interest in the work of individual students and was a frequent visitor to the classrooms; one account describes how he went softly round 'like a white moustached rabbit, with a quick, dark eye . . . .'.[15] A sense of adventure pervaded the premises at 316 Regent Street:

> 'all, staff and students alike, were united in their love for him. His staff, it was said, never felt that they were working under him, but with him. Even the students felt themselves to be pioneers taking part in an exciting experiment'.[16]

Although the syllabus in the School's first year had concentrated on subjects associated with the building trade and silversmithing, Lethaby was left free to expand the range of courses according to his own interests and in response to student demand. Classes in bookbinding, woodcuts in colour and embroidery were added in the second session; enamelling, dressmaking, writing and illuminating and printing appeared soon after. The School's work attracted international attention, 'inquiring visitors from France and Italy have been over to inspect the school, its plan and the lines upon which it is worked. There is at present no school in Paris like it.'[17] And the TEB was frequently approached for examples of student work for exhibitions abroad.[18] But however exciting, there was also a sense of the temporary and makeshift; the two buildings in Regent Street and Little Portland Street were linked by a domed conservatory with a roof that always leaked. And one student remembered that in wet weather the audience at Halsey Ricardo's architecture lectures had to take notes under opened umbrellas. The evident success of the School, the growing numbers of students, all called for a new and larger home.

In 1901 the Corporate Property Company had offered a site created by the construction of the Southampton Row extension which was to link up with the new Kingsway; the site measured approximately 10,000 square feet and the price was £45,000. The LCC agreed to the purchase and in May appropriated the site to the TEB for the new Central School of Arts and Crafts; the LCC chief architect, W.E.Riley, assisted by a team of LCC architects, took charge of the design of the building. For purposes of economy, it was decided to erect two contiguous buildings on the site: one for the Central School of Arts and Crafts (with its entrance on Theobald's Road), the other for the London Day Training College for teachers, with an entrance on Southampton Row. The two institutions were kept entirely separate, and even today with the Central occupying both, it is possible to discern the external division between the two buildings on the Southampton Row façade. But as the Training College functioned mainly during the day and the Central School in the evenings, they were able to share some of the facilities, such as the lecture theatre and refreshment room. Lethaby's thoughts on the new building, which he submitted to the TEB, were to be particularly influentia! on the final design:

> 'The whole of my experience under the Board has shown me the
> desirability of making the craft schools, as far as possible,
> representative of given industries or groups of allied industries; it
> makes the work much more real, and attracts the youths in the several
> trades.'[19]

He wished to group the subjects taught into four or five departments (suggesting schools of silversmithing and metal working, bookbinding and book production, building design and decoration, cabinet work and textiles, modelling and carving) and for each department to occupy one floor of the building. As to general appearance, he stipulated that the building should be plain, reasonable and well built.

In its last year in Regent Street the Central School had housed 126 day and 732 evening students, in addition to 22 boys who attended a day technical school in silversmithing. The small number of day students attended classes apparently especially created for women in subjects such as lacemaking, miniature painting and embroidery; the day technical students were boys who started a craft course at 13 or 14 while at the same time continuing their general education. Once moved to the new Holborn building, the attendance in 1909–1910 included 354 day and 1188 evening students, the Royal Female College of Art (recently moved from decaying

premises in Queen's Square), and two day technical schools –
silversmithing and book production. The Central School of Arts and Crafts
was no longer an experiment – it had entered the realms of the educational
establishment.

Lethaby had drawn on his many contacts with the Arts and Crafts
movement (through his membership of organisations such as the Arts and
Crafts Exhibition Society and the Art-Workers' Guild) in choosing his staff
and had succeeded in engaging a considerable number of sympathetic
designers and craft workers. This resulted in a remarkably coherent
attitude throughout the School. In the architecture department, for
example, Halsey Ricardo stated unequivocally:

> 'I am afraid you must not come to us to learn "styles", for we are a
> very practical and elementary class, I assure you. We approach the
> subject entirely from the builder's point of view; that is to say, we
> base our designs on necessity ... We don't profess to study beauty of
> form and decoration as such; whatever beauty we may gain is such as
> springs naturally out of utility, and perhaps, that is the surest way of
> teaching beauty.'[20]

The projects set in this department were formulated accordingly. For
example, one specified 'an English Catholic Church in a poor London
suburb. Materials, brick and ferro-concrete. Stone or terracotta may be
used sparingly. Cost not to exceed £6,500.'[21] The classes in lead work (a
subject of particular interest to Lethaby) run by Francis W. Troup and
William Dodds, a plumber, instructed students in every aspect of
functional plumbing, along with the history of decorative leadwork. But
one problem frequently encountered by the staff was the difficulty students
experienced in moving from their daytime, routine work to the more
challenging environment of the Central:

> 'Most of them are employed in shops where they are simply pinned
> down to one kind of work day after day without the slightest variety,
> and absolutely no scope for an idea of their own ... When he first
> came here, and had tools and metals given him to use as he pleased,
> he simply didn't know what to do with them. But now for the first
> time in his life, he is beginning to feel the handicraft under his
> fingers.'[22]

Although Lethaby encouraged the various handicrafts, he did not reject
mechanisation; for him, crafts were a vital necessity within an
industrialised society:

> 'The typical form of human industry is handiwork; thus fine writing is
> the basis for all printing. Type might have the thicks and thins in any
> positions, but that is settled by the pen in hand; the forms of vases

and pots have been decided by "throwing" the clay, the machine is quite prepared to make them like boots . . .'[23]

Lethaby realised that some craft traditions were already virtually lost, and in his determination to keep alive, and where necessary resuscitate the crafts, the Central School was to play an extraordinarily important rôle.

One of Lethaby's most brilliant appointments was that of Edward Johnston, who had visited him in 1898 as a young student of calligraphy. To his own astonishment, Johnston soon found himself in charge of the new class in writing and illuminating at the Central. These must have been some of the most exciting classes in the School, as Johnston did not attempt to hide from his students the fact that he was himself gradually (and with constant encouragement and advice from Lethaby) recreating the techniques of the craft. Johnston's influence was enormous: brilliant young students such as Noel Rooke and Eric Gill claimed that Johnston altered the whole course of their lives; foreign pupils returned to open classes in Johnston's tradition in their own countries, and he was particularly influential in Germany. His impact on book production and printmaking was profound. In the trajectory of Johnston's career, from his study of medieval manuscripts in the British Museum to the designing of his block-letter alphabet for the London Underground, we find the embodiment of Lethaby's vision of the relationship of handicraft to modern society. The calligraphy and illuminating classes were perhaps the most dramatic example of this mission to revive lost or dying crafts and pass them on to a younger generation; similar instances, however, could be found throughout the School: May Morris's instruction in embroidery, the extremely popular classes in bookbinding using tools made by Douglas Cockerell himself, Alexander Fisher's revitalising of the art of enamelling and the exciting classes in colour wood-block printing based on Japanese techniques pioneered by Frank Morley Fletcher.

Although he had to bear the main administrative load, Lethaby's position as Principal remained part-time throughout his career at the Central School. He also continued to act as art adviser to the LCC. He had accepted the Professorship of the School of Ornament and Design at the Royal College of Art in 1900 and carried out these duties concurrently with his work at the Central. In 1906 he was appointed Surveyor of Westminster Abbey, a position he no doubt cherished for its architectural and scholarly opportunities. His eventual resignation as Principal in 1911 at the age of 54 was probably partly due to the burden of these other responsibilities. He must have felt increasingly constrained by the growing bureaucracy involved in managing a large institution; the liberal and far-sighted

NOTES

I am grateful to Godfrey Rubens for much helpful advice and information and to Rosemary Heath for her assistance at the GLC History Library.

1 N.Pevsner, *Academies of Art Past and Present*, 1940, p.265 from *Die Krisis im Kunstgewerbe*, ed. R.Graus, 1901.
2 *The Studio*, special autumn number, 1916, p.20.
3 Quoted in *Technical Education for Women and Girls at Home and Abroad*, published by the Women's Industrial Council, 1905, p.41.
4 H.Llewellyn Smith, *Report to the Special Committee on Technical Education being the Result of an Enquiry into the needs of London with regard to Technical Education*, LCC, 1892, p.26.
5 *Technical Education Board Minutes*, 1896, p.156.
6 *LCC Technical Education Gazette*, Sept. 1896, Vol. II No. 23, pp.159–160.
7 'Counsel to Councils', *Punch*, October 10, 1896, p.180.
8 E.Wood, 'The School of Arts and Crafts', *The Architectural Review*, Vol. II, 1897, p.242.
9 A.R.N.Roberts, *William Richard Lethaby*, 1957, p.31.
10 *The Builder*, March 25, 1921, p.379.
11 W.R.Lethaby, 'Art and Workmanship', *The Imprint*, January 1913, reprinted in *Form and Civilization*, 1922, p.209. Lethaby went on to say: 'Every work of art shows that it was made by a human being for a human being. Art is the humanity put into workmanship, the rest is slavery.'
12 W.R.Lethaby, 'Education for Industry', *Handicrafts and Reconstruction*, 1919, p.81.
13 *Technical Education Board Minutes*, 1899, p.169
14 W.R.Lethaby, *op. cit.*, 1922, pp.211–212.
15 A.R.N.Roberts, *op. cit.*, p.30.
16 P.Johnston, *Edward Johnston*, 1976, p.98.
17 *The Artist*, May–August 1898, p.121.
18 For example: the Industrial Museum in Copenhagen, 1899; the General Association of Swedish Bookprinters, Gothenburg, 1900; Dresden, 1900 and the International Exhibition of Decorative Art, Turin, 1902. Students also figured prominently in British exhibitions such as the Earl's Court Women's Exhibition, 1900; the Glasgow International Exhibition, 1901 and the Exhibition of Arts and Crafts and Industries, Alexandra Palace, 1903.
19 *Technical Education Board Minutes*, 1903, p.111.
20 E.Wood, *op. cit.*, pp.243–4.
21 *Building News*, Sept. 23, 1910, Vol. XCIX, p.426.
22 E.Wood, *op. cit.*, p.286.
23 W.R.Lethaby, 'Introductory', *op. cit.*, 1919, p.4.
24 F.V.Burridge, *LCC Central School of Arts and Crafts, its Aim and Organisation*. Report by the Principal, 1913, p.10.
25 See *LCC Minutes of Proceedings*, 1911, pp.269–270 and Report by the Education Officer, LCC, *Eight Years of Technical Education and Continuation Schools (Mostly evening work)*, Dec. 1912, p.49.
26 W.R.Lethaby, 'Introductory', *op. cit.*, 1919, p.2.

Technical Education Board had been closed by 1904 and the LCC Education Committee did not allow him the freedom of the early Regent Street days of the School. On his resignation it was decided that the School now needed a full-time Principal. F.V.Burridge, former head of Liverpool School of Art, was appointed and remained at the Central until 1930.

At the time of Lethaby's departure, both Burridge and the LCC were keenly aware of the need for the School to maintain its links with industry and the trades. The new Principal intended to continue Lethaby's policies in so far as 'tuition should be to further the highest development of the artistic handicrafts, their application to manufacture, and their commercial usefulness'.[24] And as none of the LCC schools offered full day instruction for industrial students, he hoped to expand day teaching at the Central. The LCC too had high hopes for what it regarded as its most prestigious art school. Since the move to the new building, the Council had harboured ambitions for the Central to become the crafts and industrial art equivalent of the Royal Academy and the Slade School in fine art and looked forward to the day when the School would have university status and incorporate postgraduate work.[25]

The Central School has achieved much in terms of status, but staff and students today must confront the same issue which preoccupied the School's founders in 1896 – the rôle of the hand-crafted in an industrialised society. It is Lethaby's thinking on this question which perhaps constitutes his most valuable legacy. He believed it is at our own peril that we discard crafts for more fashionable or apparently efficient solutions. Nor was he impressed by arguments of economic viability:

'Even if it were all a question of "supply and demand" we may surely be allowed to consider what our demand is to be; unless the men who repeat this rather battered phrase mean that intelligence and will are disturbing elements and that proper "economic" demand must be entirely uninstructed and fortuitous.'[26]

New inventions should not, he felt, inevitably obliterate earlier means: every medium and technique embodies a distinct and unique means of thought and creation. In this sense, Lethaby was a great conservationist. But at the same time he chastised those who collected antiques and closed their eyes to the works of modern design as this would inevitably stifle creativity. This, then, is the challenge Lethaby has left us – the reconciliation of the insights derived from our craft traditions with a critical understanding of the advances of modern technology.

W. R. Lethaby and the Art-Workers' Guild

by John Brandon-Jones

'No great art', said Lethaby, 'is only one man deep.' He believed that progress must come by building up on what had been done before, by trying to understand the work of our predecessors and improving upon their experiments, learning from their successes and taking warning from their failures. As an architect, Lethaby's output was small, no more than three or four houses, a block of offices, one church and a number of designs for furniture and decorative work, mainly carried out by the Morris Firm; his major contribution was made through his writing and his lectures, as Principal of the Central School and as Professor of Ornament and Design at the Royal College of Art. There can be no doubt that William Richard Lethaby was one of the men who, in this century, had the most to teach his fellow architects and craftsmen.

Lethaby was always proud of his West Country origin. He began his architectural training in his native town of Barnstaple in the office of Alexander Lauder and, after working for a short time in the Midlands, he came to London to join the staff of Norman Shaw. In London, he soon established himself as the leader of a group of young architects who later formed the nucleus of the Art-Workers' Guild. Soon afterwards he made the acquaintance of Philip Webb, friend and partner of William Morris, and became his devoted disciple.

At this time 'Gothic' was still the preferred style for all major buildings, Scott and Butterfield were leaders of their profession and Bodley was on his way to the top. Shaw and Webb had both worked under G.E.Street and Morris had spent a short period in the same office. The theories propounded by Pugin and Ruskin were still fresh and exciting and it was from this base that Lethaby and his friends started to develop their own ideas.

When Lethaby wrote, 'Nothing done for the LOOK looks well', he was echoing Pugin's saying that 'An edifice which is arranged with the principal view of looking picturesque is sure to resemble an artificial waterfall or a

made up rock, which is so un-naturally natural as to appear ridiculous.'
Lethaby would also have accepted Pugin's principle that 'There shall be no
features of a building which are not necessary for convenience, construction
and propriety'.

An important milestone was the foundation, in 1884, of the Art-Workers'
Guild. It was set up by five young architects, Gerald Horsley,
W.R.Lethaby, Ernest Newton, Mervyn Macartney and W.S.Prior; all were
members or former members of the staff of Norman Shaw. This group of
friends had been meeting informally to discuss problems of art and
building and their discussions had led them to the conclusion that, as
Macartney put it:

> 'Painters, Sculptors and Architects are in danger of settling
> permanently into three distinct professions, oblivious of one another's
> aims. A Society is wanted to restore their former union with one
> another, with a programme of cohesion such as the Royal Academy
> hardly now suggests, and which the Institute of British Architects has
> deliberately rejected.'

In the same vein, Lethaby wrote: 'The drifting apart of Architecture,
Painting and Sculpture is shewn on the one hand in the trade decorations
of our buildings, and on the other in the subject painting and portrait
sculpture of our galleries. But any real Art-revival can only be on the lines
of the unity of all the aesthetic arts.' The background to these ideas can
certainly be found in the teaching of Pugin, Ruskin and Morris.

The next step in the formation of the Guild was to invite a number of
artists and craftsmen to join in the discussions and to set up a society of
painters, sculptors, architects, designers and craftsmen. The objective was
to spread a knowledge of principles among the several trades and to bring
about a better understanding of one another's arts among the members of
the society. The Guild has tried to follow the same general programme
from that day to this, but it has always had a tradition of working quietly
behind the scenes; Guildsmen have discussed their affairs together and
have then attempted to get their ideas accepted by the appropriate
professional or sectional bodies.

The first Master of the Guild was a sculptor, George Blackall Simonds; he
was followed by the architect, J.D.Sedding, and by Walter Crane, painter
and illustrator. The first honorary secretaries were Mervyn Macartney and
Gerald Horsley, both members of the founding group from Shaw's office,
and among those who joined during the first year were Lewis Day, Henry
Holiday, Basil Champneys, Beresford Pite and C.F.A.Voysey.

In 1888, the craftsmen members of the Guild, having given up all hope of persuading the Royal Academy to admit their work, decided to set up their own Arts and Crafts Exhibition Society and this still continues under the name of the Society of Designer Craftsmen. The early exhibitions held by the Society, under the presidency of Walter Crane, proved extraordinarily successful in disseminating the ideals of the Guild both in Britain and on the Continent.

At the same time, the architect members of the Guild were turning their attention to the shortcomings of professional training. The Royal Institute of British Architects had become deeply split on the question summed up in the phrase 'Architecture: a profession or an art?', which was used as the title of a book of essays published in 1892 under the editorship of Norman Shaw and T.G.Jackson. Attempts were then being made to pass an Architect's Registration Act, under which admission to the Register would be by examination. Shaw and Jackson, both members of the Academy and architects of repute, were leaders of a movement against the Bill. They believed that it was impossible to test the quality of an architect, or any other artist, by an examination.

Opposition to the Registration Act was not limited to members of the Art-Workers' Guild. Among those who signed a protest to the President of the RIBA were some distinguished and formidable figures including Butterfield, Bodley, Bentley and Webb. In fact, it would hardly be an exaggeration to say that all the architects of the period for whom we now have any respect were opposed to registration. As a result of this opposition the Bill failed in Parliament, and it was not until the 1930s that registration eventually came into force.

Meanwhile the Institute continued to experiment with a voluntary examination leading to Associate Membership, and in 1904 a Board of Architectural Education was set up to lay down a syllabus for the schools of architecture which were then being established as an alternative to articled pupillage. Horsley, Macartney, Newton and Prior were among those who had resigned from the Institute on the issue of registration. Champneys, Jackson and Lethaby had never been members, but when they realised that the problem of architectural education was being taken seriously, and that the schools had come to stay, they decided that it would be wise to go back to the Insitute and to take an active part in the work. Thus it came about that the new Board of Architectural Education had a strong contingent representing the Guild. Lethaby, as usual, took a leading part and I have it on the authority of the late Sir Ian Macallister that, although the first RIBA

Syllabus of 1906–7 appeared over the signatures of Reginald Blomfield and John Slater as Honorary Secretaries, it was in fact mainly based on Lethaby's draft. This Syllabus is a key document that should be better known.

The Board recommended that a student should have to produce satisfactory evidence of general education and some capacity in drawing. The course was to consist of at least four years' work – two years' preliminary study in the school to be followed by two years in an architect's office as a pupil or assistant – and the training was to be kept under supervision by the Board during the whole four years' term. While working in the office, the student would continue to attend lectures and would do a certain amount of work in his school. At the end of the course, he would be required to produce a study analogous to the thesis submitted for degrees in certain university courses. This was to be a study of an architectural project with working drawings and an analytical account of the nature and intention of the design. A Certificate would be awarded on completion of the course and this would be endorsed by the architect under whom the pupil had served his time.

The teaching should be governed by the principle that construction is the basis of architecture and its co-relative principle that architecture is the interpretation of construction into forms of aesthetic value. The student should be trained primarily in construction, in the composition of form and the use of materials best adapted to meeting a given problem without regard to distinctive styles. The intention was to familiarise the student with the actual facts of building, and to train him to use his brains in dealing with building. Training in the workshop and in the laboratory was to be an essential part of the course, and mathematics and applied science were to be included, but limited to the minimum indispensable for practical purposes.

As a supplement to the practical side, students should undertake studies of historic buildings of various periods so that they would be furnished with materials upon which their minds could work by analogy. They would thus be introduced to forms of proven efficiency and the genesis of these forms in constructional and social conditions would be explained so that they would come to understand that legitimate architectural form is the result of the application of the intelligence to actual and specific problems. Direct copying of known examples and deliberate attempts to reproduce specific phases of historical styles should be discouraged. In conclusion it was pointed out that it was obviously impossible to train a complete architect in four years and that all that could be done was to lay a sound foundation and to start the student on lines of study that would enable him to obtain proficiency later.

Parts of this Syllabus were put into practice in the early days of the schools; but, unfortunately, many important points were neglected and the whole movement, initiated by the Arts and Crafts group, was overtaken and overlaid by a new classical revival. The result was that several generations of students were encouraged to design by direct copying, of precisely the kind that Lethaby had warned against.

In the architectural pronouncements of the disciples of William Morris, and especially those of Lethaby and Voysey, the emphasis was on craftsmanship and through all their teaching we find that the reference is more often to matters of detail than to the design of the building as a whole. They were reacting, as every generation does, against the weaknesses of their immediate predecessors and, at the time, they had good reason to feel and speak as they did. Because they were artists of genius and had an instinct for proportion and rhythm, Morris and Lethaby took it for granted that any designer, conscientious in the pursuit of fitness for purpose and sound construction would automatically produce work of beauty.

Although they disdained both the orthodoxy of the Neo-classical and the historicism of the Gothic Revival, they did in practice rely on the support of long and careful studies of traditional buildings of all periods; but this background knowledge had been absorbed to the point at which it had become unconscious. From their studies they derived a wide vocabulary of detail and of construction which they applied to the problems of design. Many buildings designed by Lethaby and other members of the school of Webb and Shaw are completely satisfactory. But later architects with less talent or less experience made some dreadful mistakes.

The success of the Arts and Crafts architects depends upon the fact that the observer is never allowed to feel that the main components have escaped from the control of the designer, even though there is considerable freedom in the placing of minor elements. This informality, which would be out of place in a monument like the Parthenon or St Paul's, gives a touch of homeliness to the houses of Shaw or Webb or Voysey that is extremely attractive to the average English man or woman, who finds the cool correctness of the Palladians or the austerity of Soane a trifle awesome.

It is easy to see why Arts and Crafts architecture rapidly gained popularity and was taken up with enthusiasm in Europe and America as well as in Britain. It looked so simple, and the leaders, in their writings and lectures, gave the impression that if you took care of the details the masses would take care of themselves. Novelties and personal idiosyncrasies derived from Shaw or Voysey had a spell of popularity with fashionable designers but were hastily dropped when they were taken over by speculative builders and became commonplace features of suburban estates.

The average architect found it too difficult to attack every new problem from first principles; he was worried to the limit of his capacity by questions of construction or finance and felt the need for the support of a design formula. Perhaps it was the lack of formal rules that produced a reaction leading to a return to the study of classical architecture, to the popularity of 'Banker's Georgian' and to the attempts to revive the Beaux Arts system of training which took place in the Schools of the Architectural Association and Liverpool University during the first decades of the new century.

The pendulum began to swing again when it was found that a completely formal design for a utilitarian building, or one of domestic scale, involved forced symmetry at the expense of convenience. After 1918, the emphasis on craftsmanship and fine materials disappeared. Post-war difficulties in finding skilled labour combined with financial stringency to drive architects to use more and more factory-made components and, making a virtue of necessity, they became enthusiastic about designing for prefabrication and mass production. The new catch-words were Functional Expression and Structural Expression. To their embarassment, Lethaby and Voysey found themselves hailed as 'pioneers of the modern movement'. The battle against the Revivalists had been won; but, as Lethaby wrote to Harry Peach, the result was 'only another kind of design humbug to pass with a shrug. Ye olde modernist style – we must have a style to copy – what funny stuff this art is!'

Morris had set about the improvement or revival of craftsmanship in all the arts and the encouragement of proper pride in honest work. However, both Morris and Lethaby realised that machinery, if properly used, could take over much of the drudgery and dirty work of the common labourer, thus leaving more time and energy free for the interesting and exciting aspects of designing, constructing and decorating buildings, furniture and utensils. The idea that Morris was a latter-day Luddite is completely mistaken; what he objected to was the use of machinery to produce poor substitutes for craft-work and this should be obvious to any one who has taken the trouble to read his essays on the subject; even in *News from Nowhere*, he writes of powered barges carrying heavy goods on the Thames. It was unfortunate that some of his more extreme followers took the view that there was a special spiritual grace to be obtained by spending hours hacking away with a hand tool at a job that could be done in minutes by a machine.

The great designer-craftsman Ernest Gimson had such an antipathy to machinery that he refused to have anything to do with the Design and Industries Association, although his friend Lethaby was one of its promoters and begged him to work out some simple designs for factory production at prices within the reach of the working man. Lethaby's views are well summarised in an essay on 'Art and Workmanship', published in *The Imprint* in January 1913. 'Although a machine-made thing can never be a work of art in the proper sense, there is no reason why it should not be good in a secondary order – shapely, smooth, well fitting, useful; in fact like a machine itself. Machine work should show quite frankly that it is the child of the machine; it is the pretence and subterfuge of most machine-made things which makes them disgusting.'

Gimson's answer to this argument is given in a postscript to a letter to Lethaby on 18 April 1916:
> 'You see, if I did furniture for machine shops – even though different, one of the results might be (to give a lesser reason) that customers would be satisfied with that and ask for nothing more, and not only that but under the influence of D & I pamphleteering they would enjoy the pleasant feeling of giving encouragement to the latest art movement and the most sensible and up to date thing in the trade, and their patriotic breasts would be warmed by talk of extending our country's position in the world market and capturing German trade! And one's other work might not like it! I see more than difference, I see opposition!'

The result was that, although Gimson supported the Socialist ideals of Morris, his products were available only to the comparatively wealthy.

Lethaby's proposals for machine production from first-rate models were not easily accepted by contemporary designers or industrialists on this side of the Channel, but they had a profound effect upon the work of the Scandinavians and the Germans. In a pamphlet for the Design and Industries Association, Lethaby wrote:
> 'We ought to obtain far greater results from our own originality and initiative than we have done in the past. We must learn to see the

value of our own ideas before they are reflected back on us from the Continent. English designers set the type of furniture which has spread all over Europe. The English book has very greatly influenced foreign productions. Pattern designing of all kinds has been remarkably developed here, and the English fashion in design has led the world during the last generation. Nearly all we wanted was confidence in our powers, faith in our own wares, and the ambition to make as attractive as may be even the cheapest class of goods. The things of which we have been speaking have been produced in England by a special class of enthusiasts for a small number of connoisseurs, and the large manufacturer has not seen what great possibilities there were in adapting these experiments to the larger world of machine industry.'

Drawing of Lethaby by Sir William Rothenstien (see catalogue entry 18)

William Lethaby: Keeping art ship-shape

by Peter Fuller

'From another point of view a Gothic cathedral may be compared to a great cargo ship which has to attain to a balance between speed and safety. The church and the ship were both designed in the same way by a slow perfecting of parts; all was effort acting on custom, beauty was mastery, fitness, size with economy of material.'
William Lethaby, *Architecture*

'As an example of what I mean by art where order, construction, beauty, and efficiency are all one, may I instance the Navy? We must not be content until our railways are as ship-shape as a squadron. What other arts have we that hold the same beauty of efficiency carried forward in an unconsciously developing tradition? Just two or three occur to me. Simple, well-off housekeeping in the country, with tea in the garden; Boy-scouting, and tennis in flannels. These four seem to me our best forms of modern civilization, and must serve as examples of the sort of spirit in which town improvement must be undertaken. Everybody must be interested, and it must be half drill and half game.'
William Lethaby, 'Town Tidying', *Form in Civilization*

What manner of man, one might well ask, when gazing at the West front of Chartres Cathedral, thinks of a cargo ship, or, when invited to explain what he means by art, answers, 'The Navy' – or, come to that, 'tennis in flannels'?

William R. Lethaby was born in Barnstaple, in 1857, the son of a carver and gilder. He was articled to a local architect, but, in 1879, after Norman Shaw had seen his drawings in *Building News*, Lethaby was invited to join his office. There he was involved in establishing the Art-Workers' Guild, and the Arts and Crafts Exhibition Society. After ten years, he left Shaw to set up as an architect on his own.

Lethaby continued to associate himself with 'Arts and Crafts' activities. He

32

joined with Ernest Gimson to found the ill-fated Kenton and Company to make furniture; he produced interior decoration designs for William Morris and Co., and was active in the Society for the Protection of Ancient Buildings. Soon after, he became first Principal of the London Central School of Arts and Crafts. But for someone who elevated 'doing' above all else, Lethaby put up precious few buildings himself. One of the six for which he was responsible, however, was a masterpiece. Brockhampton church, in Herefordshire, built in 1901–1902, has rightly been described as 'one of the greatest monuments of the Arts and Crafts movement'. But the construction of it proved something of a trial for Lethaby, and when it was completed he effectively ceased to practise as an architect himself, complaining that he was not adequately trained to design the modern, 'scientific' buildings he had come to admire. He wrote that if he were able to start again he would, 'eschew taste and design and all that stuff and learn engineering and hard building experience. Hardness, facts, experiments – that should be architecture, not taste.'

Despite his professed distaste for book learning, Lethaby continued to pour out a stream of polemical and historical writings about architecture and design until his death. In 1915, he associated himself with the Design and Industries Association, one of whose aims was the promotion of the idea that 'many machine processes tend to certain qualities of their own'. Nonetheless, for twenty years, Lethaby was Surveyor of the Fabric of Westminster Abbey, on which he wrote a number of scholarly and anecdotal works. Predictably, by the time of his death in 1931, he was disillusioned with the Modern Movement, whose English John the Baptist on the banks of the Thames he had once seemed to be.

In retrospect, for all his considerable achievements, Lethaby's life and work seem confused and confusing. Indeed they only really begin to make sense if one acknowledges that he was trying to straddle two very different, and in most respects, opposed traditions.

One of these was the vigorous, indigenous, British critical tradition which emerged in response to spreading industrialisation in the nineteenth century. This tradition was united only in its belief that modern industrial capitalism was degrading human work, and was inimical to the fullest development of the potentialities of most individuals; in other words, it threatened personal, social and cultural life alike. Characteristically, the objections to capitalism tended to be ethical and aesthetic rather than purely political or economic – although the former inevitably phased into the latter.

The ethical objections were voiced by writers as diverse as Cobbett, Carlyle, and Arnold; the aesthetic – though neither of them was particularly fond of the word itself – by John Ruskin and William Morris, who later became a revolutionary Socialist. In the late nineteenth century, these aesthetic themes were developed in two distinct ways. Pater, Wilde, and the aesthetes of the 1880s and 1890s emphasised aesthetic response and its value in human experience. The Arts and Crafts movement, and related individuals and tendencies, initially, at least, stressed that the quality of human labour and its products ought to be the central question in any discussion of individual or social well-being.

Within this tradition, both the explanation as to why human labour was becoming debased, and the proposed solutions, varied widely. Ruskin undoubtedly offered the fullest and most complex answer to both questions. He believed that nature was the literal handiwork of God and that human labour, too, through its ornamental dimension, ought to be expressive of the spiritual as well as the practical values of society. 'All noble art', he wrote, 'is the expression of man's delight in God's work; not his own.'

Ruskin certainly was not against a practical approach to building: he argued that the first thing to be required of a building was that it should answer its purposes completely, permanently, and at the smallest expense. But he stressed that in the doing of this there was no Fine Art at all. He regarded ornamentation as the principal part of architecture, as opposed to mere building or construction: 'the highest nobility of a building does not consist in its being well built, but in its being nobly sculptured or painted'.

Architecture, for Ruskin, had nothing to do with practical use, or function. 'And above all', he warned, 'do not try to make all these pleasures reasonable, nor to connect the delight which you take in ornament with that which you take in construction of usefulness. They have no connection; and every effort that you make to reason from one to the other will blunt your sense of beauty, or confuse it with sensations altogether inferior to it.' Ruskin reminded his readers that 'the most beautiful things in the world are the most useless; peacocks and lilies, for instance'.

Similarly, in manufacture, Ruskin was hostile to machines, and the division of labour which necessarily went with them, because they eliminated this ornamental dimension and degraded the workman into a mere operative deprived of creativity and intelligence alike. Ruskin, of course, was not so foolish as to regard all pre-mechanical labour as joyous creation; indeed, he equated labour itself with 'the quantity of "Lapse", loss, or failure of human life'. Fallen men and women have to work because they can no longer expect the world immediately to meet all their complex needs. The value of labour, for Ruskin, lay precisely in its ambivalences and the imperfections of its products: and these were what the modern factory system was destroying.

He thought the problem was compounded by the fact that, in the nineteenth century, economic life was built on an ethic of competition rather than co-operation: one man was set against another. Work was thus not only stripped of its ornamental and spiritual heights and depths; it became the servant of, at best, practical necessity and, at worst, economic exigency, or the pursuit of profits. Ruskin was a High Tory who wanted to see the revival of a stable, hieratic, and Christian form of society in which each individual would be able to experience the spiritual dimension of labour, and to realise such creative potentialities as he or she possessed to the full.

Morris, too, saw that modern industrial capitalism was destroying the aesthetic aspects of work. Machines played a greater part in his utopian imaginings than in Ruskin's; but he always insisted they could make anything – except a work of art. He did not share Ruskin's religious beliefs and he regarded machines simply as tools which might eliminate drudgery and allow men and women to get on with the real business of creative living. If productive human work, and art, had once been effectively synonymous, they no longer were. Morris liked to talk as if there was really no great difficulty in conceiving of, or indeed actually realising, modern, secular equivalents of Gothic workmanship. Thus he looked forward to 'the noble communal hall of the future, unsparing of materials, generous in worthy ornament, alive with the noblest thoughts of our time, and the past, embodied in the best art which a free and manly people could produce'. He turned to revolutionary Marxism because he believed – quite wrongly as it turned out – that a Socialist revolution would inevitably lead to a worldly and democratic version of Ruskin's idealised, Christian state, where joyous, ornamental labour would flourish, uninhibitedly.

Lethaby inherited from Ruskin and Morris a belief in the centrality of *labour*. 'As work is the first necessity of existence', he once wrote, 'the very centre of gravity of our moral system, so a proper recognition of work is a necessary basis for all right religion, art and civilisation. Society becomes diseased in direct ratio to its neglect and contempt of labour.' Lethaby also shared Ruskin's and Morris's response to nature, and respect for tradition: and, though his reasons for doing so were rather different, Lethaby, too, greatly admired Gothic architecture. Nonetheless, his diagnosis of what had gone wrong with labour in modern times, and his ideas about how the situation might be remedied were fundamentally different from, and much more superficial than, theirs.

If Ruskin was a Christian Tory, and Morris a revolutionary Marxist, Lethaby liked to present himself as a down-to-earth, practical humanist. Work, or 'doing' as he liked to call it, was for him a mundane, or common-or-garden sort of activity. He did not like any emphasis being placed on 'the poetical content of workmanship'; and, of course, Ruskin's distinction between building and engineering on the one hand, and architecture proper, as Fine Art, was anathema to him. 'Wordy claims', he once complained, 'are often made for "Architecture" that it is a "Fine Art", and chief of all the arts.' But Lethaby maintained, this was nonsense: the Fine Arts by definition were free from the conditions of human need, but 'Any mastership in architecture depends on its universality and its service'.

'Labour, work, art', Lethaby once declared, 'really make up what should be one body of human service, but "fine art" has been trained to turn round and revile the rest for not being "aesthetic" – whatever that may be.' Historically, he explained, 'the word Art has meant work, production, making, doing, and it was not conceived that the spirit, the expression, the meaning of the several kinds of work could be separated from a residuum which without it becomes brute labour.'

The problem, as Lethaby saw it, was a growing lack of respect for sound, practical, manual labour; modern markets, and the education system, were bringing this about. 'One of the great phenomena of recent times', he wrote, 'has been a drift away from production towards dealing. We have to re-establish doing.' Similarly, 'Education has become . . . far too much a mere abstract grammar and far too bookish.' 'Much of the book education of the present time is an elaborate apology for our ignorance of all but print.' 'We cannot all take the veil and retire from the often rough productive work of the world.'

There may be some truth in Lethaby's argument here; but at times it borders on philistinism. Indeed, it ill becomes a popular polemicist, and learned architectural scholar, whose principal influence was through words and not deeds, to over-labour the superiority of the latter to the former. More significantly, the way in which Lethaby does so obscures the fact that the division between book learning and manual labour was more an effect than a cause of the crisis of labour in the modern world.

Indeed, for all his background in the Arts and Crafts movement, Lethaby consistently seems to miss the real force of the argument both Ruskin and Morris were making, which was not that there had been a change in the meaning of the word 'Art', nor yet a change in attitudes towards work (although, of course, they acknowledged that both these things had occurred). Rather, Ruskin and Morris were persistently pointing out that the nature of labour, and hence of art, was itself changing. Labour was being stripped of its spiritual and aesthetic dimensions *in reality*, and not just in terms of words and ideas. Lethaby notwithstanding, this spiritual and aesthetic dimension could not be restored simply by declaring that modern, de-aestheticised labour was art too; nor yet by arguing that the education system should take a more positive attitude towards what were becoming singularly unrewarding forms of work.

There are times when Lethaby perceives this himself. For example, he was faithful enough to the Ruskin–Morris tradition to declare that 'a machine-made thing can never be a work of art in the proper sense'. But it is an obervation he quickly skates over. What, for him, we are left wondering, was a work of art 'in the proper sense'? The Navy? Tennis in flannels? His much quoted definition – 'Most simply and generally art may be thought of as the well-doing of what needs doing' – is so vague and general as to be quite useless. If art is, as he says elsewhere, 'everything that was ever rightly done or made', then it is very hard to see why machine-made things cannot be works of art 'in the proper sense', or why machines themselves should not be regarded as the finest artists of all. And, at times, Lethaby comes close to arguing this. 'Design', he once wrote, 'is too often thought of as an inexplicable mystery, and it is difficult to get it understood that design does not necessarily mean a pattern drawn on paper, nor does it involve some strange originality; but it should be just the appropriate shaping and finish for the thing required.' We could hardly have moved further from John Ruskin; and, indeed, when he makes such comments, Lethaby seems clearly to have left behind the tradition that formed him, and to have opened the door to the 'Functionalism' of the Modern Movement.

Nothing better exemplifies the strangely reductive position into which Lethaby had worked himself than his attitude towards the Gothic architecture he so loved. Needless to say, in considering the architecture of the past, Lethaby begins by rejecting Ruskin's position. It is, he argues, quite impossible to differentiate between architecture and building; Ruskin was not really concerned with either. Architecture-building (one and the same thing for Lethaby) consists in 'the art of making chambered structures, the rearing of walls and balancing of vaults, but with the added interests of painted and sculptured stories'.

For Lethaby, good architecture is simply 'masterly structure with adequate workmanship'. Lethaby insists that the Gothic cathedrals were not designed 'as beauty' – let alone for the glory of God. Rather, they were developed 'along a line of experiment as surely as the great ocean liners were developed.' (Everything that was good, Lethaby believed, was also quite literally 'ship-shape'.) A ship, he argued, like a cathedral, was indeed decorated; but the ornament was only a sort of added extra – 'a gift over and above'. The essence of a Gothic cathedral, he insisted, was its structure, not its adornments, 'though never so beautiful'. And this structure testified to a desire to meet basic, practical needs. Gothic art, according to Lethaby, 'witnesses to a nation in training, hunters, craftsmen, athletes'. As David Watkin has rightly written, 'It would be hard to devise a more misleading interpretation of Gothic'.

For the cathedrals were buildings in which *even* the structure was ornamental, in Ruskin's sense: that is determined more by spiritual and aesthetic – rather than practical – needs. Their 'vaulted chambers' were themselves *symbolic*. If labour and architecture had always been simply a matter of common-or-garden practical necessities, then there would have been no cathedrals at all.

It is easy, however, to see how Lethaby got himself into this untenable position concerning the nature of Gothic if one reads his first, and most original, book, *Architecture, Mysticism, and Myth*. In one sense, this is a characteristically odd and often highly confused text – a mixture of arcane knowledge, fancy, speculation, and sharp insight. Lethaby's basic thesis is that the great architectural orders of the past embodied psychological and philosophical symbols; but these are not opaque to us because they lead back to certain ultimate facts lying behind all building, and indeed human existence itself. These included the similar needs and desires of men; the necessities materials imposed upon three-dimensional structures and the 'physical laws of their erection and combination'; and 'on the side of style, nature'.

Uniquely in Lethaby's writing, *Architecture, Mysticism, and Myth* concentrates upon the issue of style. Effectively, Lethaby tries to argue that there is a natural symbolism of architectural forms rooted in what is common to human experience in all cultures and at all times: because the men of Egypt loved the same sky that we also love, and shared the same need for shelter from the elements, we can appreciate their roofs and pyramids. The danger of this mode of arguing – and it is not one which Lethaby escapes – is that what is assumed to lie behind given, specific forms comes to be regarded as more important than those forms themselves. All architecture is reduced – for all its varieties – to the same set of qualities.

Furthermore, as Godfrey Rubens has pointed out, Lethaby falls silent – or almost silent – when it comes to describing that symbolic language, or style, which can reveal these underlying architectural truths for us, today. Lethaby is clear enough about what it should *not* be like:

> 'No barbaric gold with ruddy bloom; no jewels; emeralds half a palm over, rubies like an egg, and crystal spheres, can again be used more for magic than beauty. No terraced temples of Babylon to reach the skies; no gold plated palaces of Ecbatana, seven-walled; no ivory palaces of Ahab; nor golden houses of Nero with corridors a mile long; no stupendous temples of Egypt at first all embracing, then court and chamber narrowing and becoming lower closing in on the awed worshipper and crushing his imagination; these, all of them, can never be built again, for the manner and the materials are worked out to their final issue. Think of the Sociology and Religion of all this, and the stain across it, "each stone cemented in the blood of a human creature". Those colossal efforts of labour forced on by an implacable will, are of the past, and such an architecture is not for us, nor for the future.'

But when it comes to a description of what architecture is 'for us' and 'for the future', Lethaby is much less forthcoming:

> 'The message will be of nature and man, of order and beauty, but all will be sweetness, simplicity, freedom, confidence and light; the other is past, and well it is, for its aim was to crush life: the new, the future, is to aid life and train it, so that beauty may flow into the soul like a breeze.'

This is all very well; but it is also very vague, and incidentally uncharacteristically 'poetical'. It tells us nothing about the architectural language, or style, through which the sweetness and light will be made visible. Ruskin had declared, 'We want no new style of architecture. Who wants a new style of painting or sculpture? But we want *some* style.' And he had gone on to declare his continuing fidelity to a living Gothic tradition. Morris had spoken of the need to 'build up the ornamental part of life'. But Lethaby, the practical humanist, opts for neither of these solutions. He appears to have believed that it ought to be possible for architecture to express universal symbols and to meet practical needs without the mediation of any style. 'We require an active art of building', he once wrote, 'which will take its "style" for granted, as does naval architecture.' (Ship-shape as ever!) Predictably, this new styleless style would be free of ornament:

> 'After all, we must remember that beauty may be unadorned, and it is possible that ornamentation, which arises in such arts as tattooing, belongs to the infancy of the world, and it may be that it will disappear from our architecture as it has from our machinery.'

In such statements, of course, Lethaby echoes the arguments of pioneer modernists like Adolf Loos, Le Corbusier, and Frank Lloyd Wright, all of whom denigrated ornament, thought function could determine form without the mediation of taste or style, and believed, in effect, in the idea of a styleless modern style, based on the prototypes of mechanical production.

Today there are precious few who believe that this was more than rhetoric – rhetoric which was tragically implemented as modernist architectural practice. And Lethaby seems to have partially recognised this before he died. In this book on *Arts and Crafts Architecture*, Peter Davey quotes Lethaby as calling the Modern Movement 'only another kind of design humbug to pass with a shrug. Ye olde modernist style – we must have a style to copy – what funny stuff this art is'.

In one sense, it is easy to see why Lethaby should have turned away from Modernism. It has long been recognised that, in human terms, 'Functionalism' was not functional at all. Aesthetic decisions, decisions of taste, and the refusal of taste, were every bit as important in determining how a 'functionalist' building looked as the uses to which it was eventually put. The pursuit of 'ideals' of standardisation, anonymity, and the model of mechanism, rather than nature, could never have appealed, for long, to Lethaby with his enduring belief that architecture should, first and finally, meet real human needs.

Nonetheless, it is clear that Lethaby never shifted from his longing for a *true* functionalism, an architecture determined by nothing except the intention to meet such needs. And, in the end, we have to state clearly that this, too, was a chimera. It comes down to Lethaby's reduction of what human needs in fact are. Certainly, in social life, there is a need for 'cleanliness, tidiness, order . . . the right way of doing things', and all that Lethaby so greatly admired and identified with art itself. But it is one thing to say that there ought to be public lavatories, morgues, and bus shelters in our cities; and quite another to identify such things with the highest forms of architectural expression.

Lethaby never really grasped the point that both Ruskin and Morris were making: that human needs reach far beyond merely practical or physical necessities; indeed that is what is uniquely human about them. Lethaby's humanism was thus of a peculiarly impoverished kind. He was blind to the fact that when they are not corrupted, or stunted by adverse social conditions, human needs include the desire for individual, imaginative, ornamental, aesthetic and symbolic expression. We are the sort of creatures, unique in the animal kingdom, who relish illusion. Our needs can extend even to such things as awe, worship, and praise . . . Over all of which Lethaby maintains a deathly silence.

The meeting of men and women's needs includes the provision of a space for the expression of these imaginative and spiritual dimensions, within their architecture, and indeed, within their labour itself. And, historically, this was the function of ornament and style. Lethaby could never grasp this, which is why, in the end, there is a genteel, drab, uniformity about the trim, tidy world he keeps proposing to us. But Boy-scouting, good housekeeping, tea in the garden, naval architecture, and tennis in flannels are matters of taste, too. Of stunted taste. I, for one, would prefer, to put it mildly, a rather more Rococo style of social and cultural life.

And yet, when all is said and done, it must be admitted that Lethaby correctly perceived that once the shared symbolic order of a kind religion historically provided has disappeared, full ornamental, aesthetic, and spiritual life becomes virtually impossible. His 'solution' was simply to collapse the aesthetic into the practical – and to deny that human potentialities had thus been diminished. This is hardly satisfactory. But, in the half century since he died, no one has come any closer, in theory or in practice, to solving the problems of how men and women's aesthetic and spiritual needs can be met in a modern, secular, technological society. Even if we are unwilling to accept the solutions Lethaby offers, we can hardly evade engaging with the questions which he raises. Nor need we wonder too much about why he, himself, abandoned architectural practice, and gave so much of his life to surveying the fabric of Westminster Abbey – although he was not himself a believer.

Lethaby and the Myth of Modernism

by Gillian Naylor

'Modernism conceived as a style is only inverted archaeology, it will not be real until it is unconscious.'

Characteristic though it is of his values and his philosophy, Lethaby did not produce this statement for publication; it was one of the 'occasional random sayings' which his sister-in-law was in the habit of jotting down in his lifetime, and which were published, undated, together with extracts from letters and lectures after his death in 1931.[1] The sentence, nevertheless, seems to sum up Lethaby's concerns – his preoccupation with 'reality', his rejection of 'style', and, more significantly, his conviction that form was determined by evolutionary rather than revolutionary processes.

This dismissal of 'style' in favour of 'reality' in architecture and design was, of course, part of the philosophy he inherited from the Arts and Crafts movement. Like Ashbee, Lethaby, who was born in 1857, belonged to the second Arts and Crafts generation, and like Ashbee he had to confront the practical and ideological problems that had been inherent in the ideals of both Ruskin and Morris. What is significant about Lethaby, however, is the apparent shift in his attitudes round about 1910, when he seemed to abandon these ideals and adopt a more pragmatic approach which is reflected in his frequently quoted proto-Modern movement pronouncements. To the RIBA, for example, in 1910: 'What I *do* urge, in the simplest and plainest words, is concentration on practical, experimental and scientific education ... the living spell of building design can only be found by following the scientific method',[2] and in the *London Mercury* in 1920: 'Architecture ... must be a living, progressive, structural art, always readjusting itself to the changing conditions of time and place. If it is true it must ever be new.'[3] The most seemingly radical statements of this nature, however, were published in 1911, in his book on *Architecture* in the Home University Library series. The book's last chapter is on 'The Modern Position', and in it he maintains that 'architects should be trained as engineers are trained' and that 'damp, cracked and leaky architecture' must give way to houses that are 'as efficient as a bicycle'. He describes his own education as 'wasteful': 'It is absurd, for instance, that the writer should have been allowed to study cathedrals from Kirkwall to Rome and from Quimper to Constantinople; it would be far better to have an equivalent knowledge of steel and concrete construction.' And he concludes that 'the modern way of building must be flexible and vigorous, even smart and hard'.[4]

Convictions such as these, quoted, of course, out of context, seem to indicate Lethaby's rejection of the values of the Arts and Crafts movement. They also run counter to his convictions in the debates in 1891 as to whether architecture should be a 'closed' profession. Lethaby (together with Webb, Sedding, Mackmurdo, Butterfield and the majority of the architects associated with various aspects of the Gothic Revival) was one of the signatories of the letter to *The Times* which defined architecture as a 'fine art', and as such, not examinable. Lethaby also contributed a chapter on 'The Builder's Art and the Craftsman' to the book *Architecture: a profession or an art?* which was published in the wake of the controversy, and in it he writes: 'If you want to learn architecture, you must study architecture – that is architectural construction, not the gymnastics which overleap the building act. You must pry into material. You must learn the actual "I know" of the workmen. Work manually at a craft – if you begin with one you will end with many – not with a view of gaining what is called "practical experience", but to gain the power of real artistic expression in material'.[5]

This, of course, was the more familiar voice of Lethaby, who, in 'Art and Workmanship' (1913) wrote: 'Every work of art shows that it was made for a human being by a human being',[6] and who until the years before the First World War seemed to think and work within the traditions established by Ruskin and Morris.

Why then did he change, and seemingly ally himself with Gradgrind by declaring in 1907 in a letter to Sydney Cockerell: 'If I were learning to be a modern architect, I'd eschew taste and design and all that stuff and learn engineering with plenty of mathematics and hard building experience. Hardness, facts, experiments – that should be architecture, not taste . . . .'[7]

In order to understand Lethaby's apparent *volte-face* at this time it is necessary to trace the development of his theory, and his attitudes to what has now become that 'scare-word' Functionalism. Lethaby was born in Barnstaple, where his father was a carver and a gilder. When he was 14 he was apprenticed to Alexander Lauder, a local architect. Brian Thomas,

Master of the Art-Workers' Guild in 1957, was Lauder's grandson, and he gave details of his grandfather's career in the RIBA Centenary Symposium in honour of Lethaby. Lauder was architect to most of the neighbourhood's landowners, so that Lethaby was involved in the design of farm-buildings that 'had to work efficiently as an engine or a pump does'. Lauder also 'concerned himself with the training facilities for craftsmen, which in a provincial town like Barnstaple in the mid-nineteenth century must have been pretty meagre. He used to insist that all the men working on his own buildings should have an understanding of one another's craft, so that each might feel that he was building a house and not just practising carpentry, bricklaying and plumbing.'[8]

Lethaby, therefore, had a first-hand knowledge of practical craftsmanship before he began his career with Norman Shaw and his subsequent involvement in education and conservation. Obviously the theories of Ruskin and Morris had a profound influence on him. At the same time, his approach to concepts of architectural form were very different from theirs, and the introduction to the first book he published *Architecture, Mysticism, and Myth* (1891) gives some indication of the way his theory was to develop. 'Old architecture lives', he writes, 'because it had a purpose. Modern architecture, to be real, must not be a mere envelope without contents . . . if we would have architecture excite an interest, real and general, we must have a symbolism, immediately comprehensible by the great majority of spectators.'[9] This preoccupation with an 'immediately comprehensible symbolism' runs throughout Lethaby's writing. 'Any mastership in architecture depends on its universality and its service', he wrote in *Form in Civilization* (1922). 'We have to begin again and look on architecture as an art of service from the communal point of view'.[10] The humanitarianism inherent in the writing of Ruskin and Morris is maintained, but their stress on the demonstration of individualism in design and architecture is replaced by a concern for universality. Again, whereas Ruskin and Morris, in their attempts to preserve and maintain the vernacular tradition in British architecture, tended to look to a Gothic or medieval past, Lethaby believed that 'the development of building practice and ideas of world structure acted and re-acted on one another'.[11] The sources for the ideals and fables put forward in *Architecture, Mysticism, and Myth*, were, as Godfrey Rubens points out 'wide and indiscriminate'; they ranged from Flammarion, Grimm, Hakluyt, Petrie and Portal to Ruskin, and included Sir James Frazer's *The Golden Bough* as well as Herbert Spencer's 3-volume *The Principles of Sociology*. What is significant about this eclecticism is its stress on archaeology and mythology, and its inclusion of Spencerian sociology. The study of architecture within this cosmic context led Lethaby to conclude that the forms of architecture mirrored the values of the society that produced them. This, of course, was by no means a new concept – it was part of the canon of the Arts and Crafts movement. But while Morris came to believe that society itself must change or be changed in order to restore 'reality' to architecture and design, Lethaby, in spite of his Morris-inspired Socialism, adopted a more complex theory of the development of forms, which he conceived as a 'response to the natural conditions and psychology of their times'.[12]

Lethaby, of course, was by no means the first design theorist to put forward this point of view. Gottfried Semper, the refugee architect from Dresden, developed similar ideas in the books and articles he wrote following the Great Exhibition in 1851, when he was involved with the Schools of Design in London, and the organisation of what was then the South Kensington Museum.[13] Style, according to Semper, was determined by the available materials and tools, the climate, the customs, and above all the symbolic requirements of any given society. Style, therefore, followed evolutionary laws, a theory which Semper developed further when he saw Cuvier's collection in the Jardin des Plantes in Paris: 'In this magnificent collection . . . we perceive *the types* for all the most complicated forms of the animal empire, we see progressing nature, with all its variety and immense richness, most sparing and economical in all its forms and motifs. A method, analogous to that which Cuvier followed applied to art, and especially architecture, would at least contribute to getting a clear insight over its whole province, and perhaps also form the basis of a doctrine of *style* and a sort of *topic*, or method, of how to "invent".'[14]

The consequences of such theories are obvious – they recur in the writing of Viollet-le-Duc, and re-emerge in the twentieth century with Corbusier's and Gropius' preoccupation with 'type-forms'. It is not certain that Lethaby read Semper, but he certainly read Viollet-le-Duc, as well as Herbert Spencer, and it was his wide-ranging historical studies, his interest in biological and social analogies, and his concern for the future of architecture that led him to his seemingly radical attitudes, and his preoccupation with the *language* rather than the appearance of form. 'The Architecture of Adventure', a paper he gave to the RIBA in 1910, shows Lethaby in the process of formulating his position.[15] He describes how the 'styles' of the past – Greek, Roman or Gothic – were achieved through a unity of the arts in the relevant periods, so that 'all expressed their thought in a common current language'. The problem was to develop a contemporary architectural language: 'However desirable it might be to continue in the old ways or revert to past types, it is, I feel on reviewing the attempts that have been made, impossible. We have passed into a scientific age, and the old practical arts, produced instinctively, belong to an entirely different era.' In the past, he maintains, architects were engineers, and in England, Christopher Wren – 'a great intellect most wholly trained in all the science and philosophy of an ample age' – was the first 'to apply the methods of scientific investigation to the laws of structure', and to express these laws through geometry and proportion. Equivalent studies, appropriate to contemporary research, should be undertaken to establish a 'method of design' that 'would reconcile again Science with Art'. 'The method of design to a modern mind can only be understood in the scientific or engineer's sense, as a definite analysis of possibilities – not as a vague poetic dealing with poetic matters, with derivative ideas of what looks domestic, or looks farmlike, or looks ecclesiastical – the dealing with a multitude of flavours – that is what architects have been doing for the last hundred years.'

This essay, therefore, is a key statement of Lethaby's theories prior to the First World War, and it demonstrates the ideological impasse he had reached. He describes the 'old practical arts' as 'instinctive', thus rejecting any conscious contribution from the designer; he (like Mackmurdo before him) rehabilitates Wren, the scientist and mathematician whose achievements were denigrated by Morris, because Wren applied the 'objective' knowledge of science and geometry to architectural form, and he dismisses the achievements of the nineteenth century as 'derivative', too rooted in associationism to be 'real'.

Obviously Lethaby could not describe the forms the new architecture was to take – he could only assume that they should be determined by the 'scientific method', thus expressing the spirit of the age. By adopting this position Lethaby was following the approach first established in this country by Semper, and it is ironic that the founder of the Central School, that bastion of Arts and Crafts ideals, should come to express theories implicit in the 'methodologies' of the Schools of Design. There is no evidence that Lethaby attempted to apply any objective 'method' in his teaching at the Central School, but he was, like his predecessors, faced with the problem of how and what to teach. This is, of course, a perennial problem, and it is no coincidence that some seventy years later, both Sir Leslie Martin in the Lethaby lecture at the Royal College of Art in 1982, and Dr Lionel March in his Inaugural as Rector of the RCA that same year, should both claim Lethaby as a pioneer of the 'systems' approach to design. The title of Dr March's lecture – *Systematic Research into Possibilities* – was taken from *The Architecture of Adventure*.

Lethaby's attempts to 'de-subjectivate' architecture in order to establish a 'scientific' and in his terms rational approach to its theory and practice have obvious equivalents in twentieth-century theory, and they have led, naturally enough, to somewhat equivocal assessments of his significance. He has, of course, been seen as a pioneer of modern design; Frank Walker, in the series of articles published on the occasion of Lethaby's centenary, said that Lethaby had the 'misfortune to be born in the wrong place at the wrong time',[16] and more recently he has been described as 'collectivist and anti-intellectual' – 'a pleasingly eccentric product of the English Arts and Crafts movement overlaid with French Rationalism'.[17] Lethaby's dilemmas are important, however, not because (*pace* David Watkin) they demonstrate the eccentricities of the English in search of a theory, but because Lethaby attempted to reconcile two traditions – the rational and the romantic – in nineteenth-century design theory. If one equates Semper with the rational tradition and Morris with the romantic, one can identify certain shared assumptions: first, that architecture and design reflect social values and priorities; second, that form should be determined by, and expressive of the nature of materials, and third, that form should respond to emotional as well as practical needs. It is on the nature of the determinants for these traditions, however, that Semper and Morris part company. The Semperian approach implies objective and evolutionary developments, while Morris saw design and the designer as agents of social change. Lethaby would never deny the achievements of Morris – he and Webb were the champions of what Lethaby called 'reasonable building' [18] – but the Gothic Revival, with its concern for the 'appearance' rather than the 'essence' of architecture, had degenerated into a style. In place of 'style' Lethaby called for a 'new science of building morphology' – 'a true science of architecture', a 'sort of architectural biology'.[19]

By recommending a scientific and therefore objective and analytical approach to architecture, Lethaby was, in effect, rejecting the historicism and associationism of the Gothic Revival in the belief that the 'new science of building morphology' would identify certain basic principles of structure, thus ensuring the logical, rather than idiosyncratic development of architectural form. Knowledge of the history of architecture was essential, both as a means, and as an end. 'We cannot forget our historical knowledge, nor would we if we might', wrote Lethaby. 'The important question is, Can it be organised and directed, or must we continue to be betrayed by it? The only agreement that seems possible is agreement on a scientific basis, on an endeavour after structural efficiency. If we could agree on this we need not trouble about beauty, for that would take care of itself.'[20]

In the period from 1910–1920, therefore, Lethaby was attempting to formulate a theory of architecture that was based on his experience as a designer and a teacher, as well as on his historical research. The only practical demonstrations of what he might have had in mind are Brockhampton church, with its thatched roof and concrete vault, and his entry for the Liverpool Cathedral Competition (both 1902). Despite the seemingly unorthodox use of concrete, however, neither design attempts formal innovation: the Herefordshire church 'type' is confirmed in Brockhampton, and the Liverpool design demonstrates the virtuosity of concrete in the span of its traditional vault forms. For unlike the pioneers of the Modern Movement, Lethaby could never, either in theory or practice, contemplate a total break with the past. Style could not be imposed, and 'modernism' as Lethaby conceived it, could only emerge from a developing tradition. 'Modernism conceived as a style', therefore, as far as Lethaby was concerned, was only a mirage; it did not even have the potency of a myth. 'Architecture is human skill and feeling shown in the great necessary act of building. It must be a living, progressive, structural art, always re-adjusting itself to changing conditions of time and place. If it is true, it must ever be new. This, however, not with a willed novelty, which is as bad as, or worse than, trivial antiquarianism, but in response to *force majeure*.'[21]

The *force majeure* in the twentieth century, according to Lethaby, was science, but science, as he came to realise, could be manipulated into perversion as well as progress. 'Seeking isolated Truth has turned into Science', he wrote, 'which means bombing, vivisection and political economy – orthodox political economy is a creed – the theology of mammon.'[22] 'I am altogether inadequate for the methods of science', he wrote in his last book *Architecture, Nature and Magic*; the book, which was a reworking of *Architecture, Mysticism, and Myth*, was first printed in serial form in *The Builder* in 1928, when the theories of Modernism were being consolidated on the Continent; it was not published in book form until 1956, a year after the consecration of Ronchamp, a building which Lethaby would no doubt have approved of, but one which Pevsner described as 'the most discussed monument of a new irrationalism'.[23]

NOTES

1 *Scrip's and Scraps*, W.R.Lethaby, ed. Alfred H.Powell, Earle and Ludlow (printers) n.d, page 50.
2 *Form in Civilization: The Architecture of Adventure*, RIBA, 1910, *Form in Civilization*, London, 1922, pages 90–91.
3 *Ibid*. page 7.
4 *Architecture: an Introduction to the History and Theory of the Art of Building*, Home University Library, London and New York, 1911, pages 247–251.
5 *Architecture: a profession or an art?* ed. R.Norman Shaw and T.G.Jackson, John Murray, London, 1892, pages 164–5. Excerpts from the letter to *The Times* are published in the introduction, page xxxiii.
6 *Form in Civilization*, op. cit. page 210.
7 Quoted by Basil Ward; Symposium in Honour of Lethaby's Centenary, RIBA Journal, Vol. 64, April 1957, page 222.
8 Brian Thomas, *ibid*. page 218.
9 *Architecture, Mysticism and Myth*; first published 1891; Architectural Press reprint, with introduction by Godfrey Rubens, 1974, page 7.
10 *Form in Civilization*, op. cit. pages 8 and 9.
11 *Architecture, Nature and Magic*, Duckworth, London, 1956, page 15.
12 *Form in Civilization*, op. cit. page 12.
13 Gottfried Semper came to London in 1850. His essay *Wissenschaft, Industrie und Kunst* – a report on the Great Exhibition – was published in German in 1852. He was working on his major theoretical work *Der Stil in den technischen und tektonischen Künsten*, which was intended as a 'handbook of practical aesthetics' from about 1844. It was finally published in two volumes 1860–63.
14 Quoted from page 67, *The Evolution of Design*, Philip Steadman, Cambridge, 1979.
15 *Form in Civilization*, op. cit., pages 66–95.
16 'William Lethaby and his scientific outlook', Frank A. Walker, *AA Quarterly*, Vol. 9, No. 4, page 52.
17 *Morality and Architecture*, David Watkin, Oxford, 1977, pages 36 and 33.
18 *Philip Webb and his work*, W.R. Lethaby, Raven Oak Press reprint, page 65.
19 *Architecture*, op cit., page 248.
20 *Ibid*., page 248.
21 *Form in Civilization*, op cit., page 7.
22 *Scrip's and Scraps*, op cit., page 39.
23 *An Outline of European Architecture*, Nikolaus Pevsner, Penguin Books Ltd, seventh edition, 1963, page 429.

The Practice and Theory of Architecture

by Godfrey Rubens

In this short essay I have not attempted to discuss all of Lethaby's buildings but to pick out from them various themes and ideas whose significance it is vital to understand if one is to follow the development of his theories and their expression in his work. For Lethaby, architecture was the quintessential art – the matrix of civilisation. His perception of its nature and purpose changed and developed enormously throughout his life and this development was expressed in three distinct positions. The first two can be explained in his artefacts and writings, the last and most radical only in his words and actions. In the first period, which ended in about 1890, and shortly after he started in practice, his work was characterised by a wide and sensitively-used knowledge of architectural style, attempts, perhaps unconscious, to give it symbolic meaning, an abiding interest in plane and solid geometry and, in straining after originality, a deal of experiment. Three designs, for a cemetery chapel, a wayside chapel and a school, which were all produced for competitions, exemplify this period. The first, which is a classical design with Ionic pilasters, has a stark simplicity and deathlike serenity: it is exactly not what might be expected from a former pupil of Alexander Lauder, the designer of florid Gothic Revival chapels. The second, in contrast, is a more delicate invention in the Gothic style, distinguished by its more workable plan and an ingenious arrangement of bell gable and entrance porch at the west end. Finally in 1882 came the entry for the St Anne's Schools competition by M.Macartney, E.Newton and Lethaby, who was responsible for the façade design. At this time Lethaby made his first venture into architectural theory with a talk on Renaissance architecture; this proposed an extraordinary mixture of early Renaissance motifs from England, Germany and Holland as a recipe for modern design and ended with this quotation from Francis Bacon: 'there is no exquisite beauty without some strangeness in its proportion'.[1] The proposals fairly describe the bizarre mixture of Renaissance styles and strange proportions of the St Anne's design.

In the latter part of the 1880s Lethaby started to produce simpler and less wilful work, which shows the beginnings of a change of direction and is manifest in Avon Tyrrell, a large country house in the New Forest designed for Lord and Lady Manners. Its plan is testament to all that he had learned in the years in Shaw's office, but the elevations are more individual. The essentials of a great house are packed under a single roof, which gives unity and simplicity to the whole and serves as a foil for the piquant grouping of the bays, the gables, rain heads and other details which are governed by aesthetic, as much as practical considerations. The garden and entrance elevations are very different and a contrast in formal and informal arrangements. The entrance façade has a rhythm which builds up slowly from the low wall of the kitchen court to the crescendo at the other end – the great mullion and transom window, the front door and the massive twelve-sided chimney stack, a bold emblem which stands over the entrance in an almost Jacobean fashion. But the other side is quieter and has a far more even measure and is contained at one end by the projection of the drawing-room bay and at the other by a chimney breast.

'When I first had to do with the building trade', wrote Lethaby in words that sum up his work to this point, 'I thought of "designing as a mysterious gift" and awsomely hoped I had "got it" or that it would come, for it was of the nature of inspiration. One had to know something of disagreeable buildings facts, and the employer's horrid requirements, but "design" itself was the embodiment of vision by genius.'[2] The sharp change in Lethaby's ideas which took place about 1890 can be demonstrated by examining what he wrote during this time and comparing two pieces of furniture, a walnut cabinet exhibited at the 1890 Arts and Crafts Exhibition and an oak chest made by Kenton & Co. and exhibited a year later. In general form and sober elegance the cabinet looked back to the seventeenth century, but it was given a decidedly novel look by the complex curvilinear mouldings that were applied to its four doors. The chest differs from it in two fundamental ways; it was constructed by a different system of solid wood with exposed dovetails and was quite unlike the other, which concealed both construction and carcase under a layer of veneer. Furthermore, its decoration was not, like the mouldings of the cabinet, applied to the surface, but inlaid into the solid wood. The real significance of these differences comes out first in an angry attack on modern labour conditions and building practice, in which he quoted John Ruskin on the evils attendant upon the division of labour and its separation of thinking from doing, and designer from maker.[3] Second is a surprising talk on carpenters' furniture given at the Arts and Crafts Exhibition[4] where his walnut cabinet was on show: surprising, because in it he praised very simple unsophisticated furniture entirely different from his own both in style and construction. Furthermore, it was made and designed by the same man and not, therefore, the product of divided labour. Now although in appearance the oak chest looks far more like a piece of carpenters' furniture than does the cabinet, that in itself is not enough to explain the significance of these differences or why they took place.

Lethaby's two essays referred to above had adumbrated much of the philosophy of the Arts and Crafts movement, which preached that true art could only be produced when designer and maker were one and the same. Hence the question that must have forced itself on him was: how was it possible to continue to design what others would make? For answers he returned to Ruskin's essay, previously referred to, where he found the clue that was to enable him to resolve the problem. Ruskin had written 'on a large scale and in work determined by line and rule it is possible and necessary that the thoughts of one man should be carried out by the labour of others'.[5] What Lethaby did, of course, was to apply Ruskin's principle to small-scale work and in a way that the latter could scarcely have conceived of, and it is this which explains the differences between the cabinet and the chest. The first, with its complex mouldings, carcase and veneer, was obviously the product of divided labour and several craftsmen as well as a designer, but the second, being determined by 'line and rule' and no more than 'the putting together of material'[6] which was enriched with a simple inlay was apparently not.

It is these changes in Lethaby's theory which explain most of the differences between Avon Tyrrell and The Hurst built in 1893 at Sutton Coldfield for Charles Matthews, a Birmingham solicitor. The design of the latter was a conscious (perhaps even self-conscious) effort to make the elevations express the plan, that is to say the forms and functions of the spaces within. The decoration was either mathematically determined, like the forms of the superb chimney pieces, made from carefully chosen marble rectangles, or was executed by a free craftsman, in this case Lethaby, who modelled the plaster friezes, the ceiling decoration and some terracotta panels for the exterior.

In 1898, Thomas Middlemore, a retired Birmingham businessman who had bought a large estate in the Orkneys, employed Lethaby to build him a medium-sized country house on the island of Hoy. This was at Melsetter where there stood a miscellaneous collection of buildings – a laird's house, a steading and various other structures. By a brilliant piece of planning which preserved much of what was already there, Lethaby turned them into a coherently organised country house. A new steading or farmyard was built some distance away and the old one made into a walled rose garden.

The new work, of a higher standard of craftsmanship than the old, was, with the exception of the splendid ashlar chimneys, constructed of harled and whitened rubble sandstone in the traditional way, but the trims to the new windows and doors have Orcadian roll mouldings, which are enough to distinguish them from the old ones. By thus separating his work from that of the original builders Lethaby enables much of the outline of the old house to be traced within the new.

If, in their buildings, English architects of the nineteenth century used iron or concrete at all, they were almost inevitably concealed behind façades of stone or brick, which, with wood, were considered the only true materials for the creation of 'Architecture'; furthermore, most of them lacked the technical knowledge to use either iron or concrete, even if they had wanted to. Yet there were a few, mostly in the Arts and Crafts movement, who saw these novel materials as part and parcel of modern industrial society, which, despite reservations about the social implications of their use, it was foolish and obscurantist to turn one's back on, since they opened a way to new and better construction. Lethaby started experimenting with concrete at S.S.Margaret and Colm, the chapel he built at Melsetter, where on low walls of massive random rubble, he erected a monolithic concrete vault covered with large stone slates. Despite its small size the chapel gives that strong impression of primitive power Ruskin believed was part of the essential nature of Gothic architecture. All Saints Church at Brockhampton, Ross-on-Wye, was built in 1902 and paid for by Alice Foster in memory of her parents. At first sight it looks, with its random rubble construction and thatch, typical Hereford, but this is belied by its sharp arrises and general squareness. Within the dominant motifs are the steeply pointed stone arches with a single chamfer in the nave and double at the crossing, which die directly into the imposts. They support a mass concrete tunnel vault, formed over rough boards, that was punctuated along its length by two lines of oil lamps hanging from it on long spindly rods.

Undoubtedly the work at Melsetter, successfully completed less than a year earlier, had given Lethaby the confidence and technical experience needed for this far more ambitious scheme and, another aim of Arts and Crafts architects, built not by a building contractor, but by direct labour. To protect the concrete from weathering thatch was used because it was not only cheaper, but being lighter it exerted less pressure on the shell of the vault. It has proved an excellent, if unconventional isolant, for the concrete is still in perfect condition. The interior produces a powerful evocation of a Gothic building although no Gothic forms are used and is Expressionist in the sense that European architecture was twenty years later.

In 1902 Lethaby, H.Ricardo, R.Schultz Weir and H.Wilson submitted an unconventional design, both in form and materials, for the Liverpool Cathedral Competition. Concrete was proposed for the construction and it was to be used in a way that made walls and roof all-in-one, in a corrugated form and therefore self-buttressing. The use of these forms suggests that mass rather than reinforced concrete was intended and there can be little doubt that Lethaby, who was largely responsible for the design[7]; used because, in the first place, he would only work with materials he understood and secondly, there was a great deal of uncertainty about ferro-concrete, which has since proved well founded, for a number of structures built of it at that time are showing increasing signs of failure. Mass concrete, in contrast, was very durable and therefore appropriate for a building designed to stand for generations. The design, developed from All Saints, is more sophisticated and entirely homogeneous, for plan and elevations have become inseparable and, unlike many other competition entries, it was functionally successful. The fact, however, that this most original design received no mention in the assessors' report must be due to its unconventionality and to the firm conviction that cathedrals, being 'Architecture', could be built of nothing but stone.

Lethaby sought always to give his work meaning beyond function: to enrich it with forms that symbolised ideas. As his perception of the nature of architecture and of society changed, however, so did the forms he used. At first, when he believed design to be largely a question of juggling with motifs from past styles, this desire to find appropriate symbols only breaks through occasionally, as in the cemetery chapel design previously mentioned.

Soon, however, this search became a central preoccupation which resulted in the publication of his first book *Architecture, Mysticism, and Myth* and in the use of symbols from it in his designs. To take one example which was typical of the rest: the great chimney stack, with its attendant birds standing on either side of it, above the front door at Avon Tyrrell. The significance of this arrangement can be understood by reference to Lethaby's book where he describes and illustrates a sculptural group consisting of a large egg-shaped stone, with an eagle at each side, which marked the sacred centre or omphalos of the earth at Delphi in ancient times. In his discussion of the meaning of the omphalos, the author explains how it came to be equated with the hearth and, thus, to symbolise the centre of the house and navel of the family. If, for the great stone and eagles, a chimney – the exterior expression of the hearth – and peacocks – the Manners' emblems – are substituted, the resulting invention, which brings together the epic and functional, becomes the symbolic hub and omphalos of the Manners family and thus of Avon Tyrrell itself.

Within a short time he came to see that the real problem was to create an intelligible symbolism for contemporary society and not delve into remote and esoteric sources for ideas, however much fun it might be. It was in this context that he spoke in 1894 of the need for architecture to be Expressionist, that is to say, builders had to make the interior and exterior forms expressive of the character, nature, construction, function and so on of the building – it had, in other words to symbolise its own reality. It is this desire that explains his use of such terms as 'houseright' and 'houseness' when discussing this problem.

It is in this sense that The Hurst was Expressionist where Avon Tyrrell was not, for not only do the exterior forms express the plan, but they attempt to symbolise it, as for example in the relationship of the low mansard roof of the servants' wing to the more dominant main block and in the way that the form of the Serlian window in the entrance façade is the transverse section of the groin vault of the hall behind it.

After Lethaby's appointment as first Professor of Ornament and Design at the Royal College of Art in 1901 he designed little. There were several reasons for this withdrawal: one was certainly lack of time, for he remained an LCC Chief Inspector and Principal of the Central School of Arts and Crafts; for another, he felt himself, by virtue of his training, to be entirely inadequate to build under modern conditions and in modern materials. Furthermore, his ideas were becoming increasingly unpopular in England, where the revival of various forms of classicism was in full swing. He must have realised, too, that it was more important to be involved in education and journalism where his ideas would have more influence. This explains the reason for choosing to write in *The Builder*, a popular journal with a wide circulation in the building trade, reaching an audience far beyond that of his fellow architects. For three decades, until his death, there appeared in it a constant stream of marvellous articles touching on all aspects of architecture: in many he put forward with increasing conviction and power a theory of architecture entirely different from that offered and still offered by most architectural theoreticians. Then, to give effect to his conviction that no real architecture was possible without agreement on a common programme, he founded in 1922 the Modern Architecture Constructive Group, whose members accepted this somewhat simplified version of

Lethaby's definition of architecture:

> 'Architecture should be a developing structural art mainly concerned with the building and bettering of cities and the provision of all structures required in civilization'.[8]

The Group's Manifesto stressed the need to satisfy the special requirements of the time by experiment.

Lethaby's articles criticising the architecture of his time were characterised by a gentle irony and lack of rancour, but his attacks were merciless nevertheless, and this makes it hard to understand how it came about that the RIBA, the progenitor of Beaux Arts classicism, decided to offer him their Gold Medal, but it does make comprehensible his refusal of that honour. The architectural establishment, because it viewed architecture as mainly a question of style and aesthetic experience, nevertheless succeeded, until recently, in burying Lethaby, but in the wake of the collapse of yet another style his ideas command increasing attention.

NOTES

[1] *The Architect*, 1883, p.434.
[2] *The Builder*, 1923, p.405.
[3] Lethaby, W. 'The Builder's Art and the Craftsmen' in Shaw, R.N. and Jackson, T.G. (Eds) *Architecture: a profession or an art?*, London 1892.
[4] *Arts and Crafts Essays*, pp.302–309, London 1893.
[5] Ruskin, J. *The Stones of Venice* Vol. II.
[6] *The Builder*, 1896, p.307.
[7] Schultz Weir, R. 'Willaim Richard Lethaby', A paper read before the Art-Workers' Guild, April 1932. Library of the RIBA.
[8] *The Builder*, 1918, p.213.

Architecture, Mysticism, and Myth
and its influence

by Julian Holder

'. . . this is, so far as known to me, the only attempt to set out, from an architect's point of view, the basis of certain ideas common in the architecture of many lands and religions, the purpose behind structure and form which may be called the esoteric principles of architecture.'

With these words Lethaby began the preface to his first book *Architecture, Mysticism, and Myth* published in 1891. It is a curious book and one often overlooked in the history of nineteenth-century architectural thought. However, as the dust is blown away from such key areas as the 'family', as it was known,[1] of Richard Norman Shaw's office and the Art-Workers' Guild a clearer picture of its importance becomes possible.

At the time of publication Lethaby had been in private practice for a little over two years, after nearly ten as Shaw's chief assistant. He was 34, a devoted reader of Ruskin, and an admirer of Richard Phené Spiers, the master of architecture at the Royal Academy. Robert Schultz Weir, one of Lethaby's closest friends, an employee of Shaw, and member of the Art-Workers' Guild, tells us of the Saturday afternoons they spent sketching together before going on to a gathering at Spiers house in the evening where '. . . we were always sure to meet interesting people'.[2]

While, as Robert MacLeod has put it, 'Philip Webb begat William Richard Lethaby',[3] the theory of architecture displayed in *Architecture, Mysticism, and Myth* would seem to be incompatible with the practice of Webb. Neither does the book show Lethaby in his other chief rôle to date, as a supposed 'pioneer of the Modern Movement'. Grounds for both views can be found but they do not apply so readily to Lethaby in 1891 when he had only just met Webb. However, from that moment on it seems '. . . Philip Webb satisfied my mind about that mysterious thing we call architecture'.[4]

We may infer then that the author of *Architecture, Mysticism, and Myth* was still unclear as to '. . . the purposes behind structure . . .' when he wrote the book and was in some way trying to define the nature of architecture.

In this he was not alone, but in advancing the idea of an ahistorical symbolism as the basis of architecture he was, at this time, unique.[5]

Just as the French Revolution and the theory of evolution had destroyed the basis of social and religious life for many people, so revivalism seemed to deny any common basis for architecture. Forms had lost their original meaning. Speaking of the Royal Academy show of 1875 one reviewer had declared '. . . the age of revivalism may well be over. I for one sincerely hope that it is.' In their efforts to turn the practice of architecture into a profession many architects were eager to dissociate themselves from the building trades. This was done chiefly to secure the artistic side of the building process – design – for themselves. In reality it was all the increasing use of general contract building had left them to do.[6]

Nonetheless, once a 'new' style became fashionable, builders showed themselves more than capable of copying it. Frequent stylistic innovation then became one of the methods by which architects kept themselves employed. The reviewer of the Royal Academy show had been prompted to make this remark by the work of the then new 'Queen Anne' style. However, his wish that revivalism might be over was not granted. Richard Norman Shaw, the architect who more than any other became synonymous wth 'Queen Anne', despaired at the ease with which the style was reproduced and reverted to his own version of the Classical manner. The Byzantine,[7] English Free style, Baroque, and Georgian revivals continued the momentum of stylistic change well into the present century.

In spite of the moral imperative invariably given each style, there could no longer be any pretence that there was any 'true' style in the sense that Pugin or Ruskin writing earlier in the century would have wanted. One way out of this aridity, this lack of 'meaning' in architecture where a style that had once signified the power of princes could be applied to a railway station, an abbatoir, or an alehouse, was in the practice of the Arts and Crafts movement and the example of Philip Webb. However, in Webb's case his small output and strong distaste for publicity of any kind meant that there was little alternative to personal contact.

Architecture, Mysticism, and Myth then represents Lethaby's own attempt to suggest the way architecture could move out of the poverty of revivalism by an architecture expressing deeply held beliefs – myths – through commonly-found symbols – mysticism. As he writes in the introduction '. . . old architecture lived because it had a purpose'.

The relationship of mythical symbols to architecture is a subject which had clearly exercised a fascination for Lethaby over many years. In 1889 he gave an address to the Architectural Association entitled 'Of the "motive" in architectural design'[8] in which he was already looking for the basis of architecture beyond mere revivalism. Accordingly he complained to his audience that '. . . owing to the misdirection of energy our several powers are wasted in false issues – building correct "Early English" churches, or "Grecian" townhalls'. What he tells us of the circumstances of compiling the book also speaks of his long interest:

> 'The main proposition occurred to me after collecting and comparing a large number of architectural legends, and it was not until I read definitely for further confirmation that I found statements, a sentence here and there, anticipating me on nearly every point.'[9]

Indeed, when we read the book this 'magpie' or 'scissors-and-paste' method of composition is very evident. One of the first reviewers of the book complained that '. . . such a multiplicity of examples . . . make this book appear to be the production of a past age, when scholarship of the kind could be appreciated'.[10] Not only the scrapbook method but the amount and currency of much of his reading is also evident to the extent that he quotes from several books only recently published.[11]

On the whole the book was favourably received although *The Times* found that '. . . his insight is so esoteric that to plain people its deliverances are simply unintelligible'.[12] Nonetheless it was reprinted within a year and 'Symbolism in Art' was the topic of a meeting of the Art-Workers' Guild on 4 November 1892.

The trade press of 1891 gave fairly balanced reviews which aimed at description more than appraisal. The reviewer for *The British Architect* clearly saw the book in the context of the debate then raging to close the architectural profession by a system of examination when he commented that 'Of late we have been deluged with almost every kind of argument to prove that architecture is something that it really is not'.[13] However, apart from this one contemporary reference any possibility that such esoteric ideas could motivate architects of the day is dismissed and the work received as a solid, if quirky, work of history. Only the reviewer of the *Architectural Association Notes*,[14] as the representative of the student voice of the future generation of architects perceived the possibility of turning its theory into practice:

> 'Here lies the germ of all noble building in the future and we earnestly hope that the appearance of this book is itself a sign of the ripeness of

the times and that it comes to an expectant world able and willing to make use of the ideas it contains.'

In practice the '. . . use of the ideas . . .' in Lethaby's own work is somewhat disappointing when compared to that of some of his contemporaries. His Eagle Insurance Building, Birmingham (1900) provides one example of the way the ideas could be applied. Most obvious is the use of eagles themselves. In chapter 8 of the book, entitled 'The Golden Gate of the Sun', Lethaby tells the reader:

'When the earth, or rather the wall of mountains surrounding the utmost bounds of ocean, was the foundation of the solid sky, some contrivance was necessary to account for the disappearance and return of the sun . . . The general early view was that there were two openings – the Gates of the East, and the Gates of the West.'

Such gates, he notes, could be marked by the sculpture of an enormous eagle, as we find at the top of the Eagle Insurance Building. The original design for the building showed *two* eagles which would also have symbolised the subject of chapter 4, 'At the centre of the earth', for the '. . . story was told that to determine the true centre of the earth, Jupiter sent out two eagles, one from the east, the other from the west, and they met at this spot'. With the eagle symbolising the sun it is possible to read the curious design of the parapet, with its triangular, circular, and semi-circular forms, as a symbol for the firmament through which the sun travels beneath the rippled cornice symbolising the oceans that enclosed the earth. Similarly the highly polished doors of the two entrances, with discs representing the sun, become the sun gates of east and west for '. . . when the churches were entered opposite the setting sun, the power of the old symbolism was lost, but it survived long, if largely unconsciously. Right into the Middle Ages shining metal was the only fit material for the doors of entrance.'

A similar pattern is discernible in the first commission of fellow Art-Workers' Guild member Charles Harrison Townesend. This was the Bishopsgate Institute (1892–4). It is one of a group of buildings designed for charitable foundations and movements such as the Free Public Libraries which seem to have favoured the more progressive designers of the 1890s. At Bishopsgate the symbolism is more overt than at the Eagle Insurance Building. The original entrance gates, now sadly destroyed, carried a large flaming sun of wrought iron above them, roughly four feet in diameter.[15] If in no other way Lethaby's position as Art Inspector for the LCC Technical Education Board gave him a considerable influence over the LCC Architects' Department. It is not surprising then to find the symbolism of the 'Golden Gate of the Sun' in the gates of its Caledonian Estate, Islington (1904).

We can see from these examples that from the ten principal chapters of the book (each treating one area of symbolism) only one or two are employed on any one building. In practice these seem to have been the idea of sun gates, trees both as symbols of life and as representations of the earliest structural members, ceilings decorated like the sky, domes to suggest tents and the firmament, patterned floors to suggest the sea, four-square windows and ground plans to suggest solidity and permanence, tortuous passages to create labyrinths, and eggs to suggest creation.

On his return from the Far East in 1891 R.W.Schultz found that '. . . the book opened up to us younger men a hitherto undreamt of romance . . . I was at that time about to do a small private chapel, into it went a pavement like the sea and a ceiling like the sky'.[16]

The symbolic intent of the chapel, built in 1893 for the third Marquis of Bute at St John's Lodge, Regents Park, was repeated in Schultz Weir's St Andrew's chapel for the fourth Marquis at Westminster Cathedral in 1912. In addition to the Bishopsgate Institute, Townesend's other notable works – the Whitechapel Art Gallery, Horniman Museum, St Mary the Virgin, Great Warely, and the design for the United Free Church, Woodford Green – all contain elements discussed in the book. Most noticeable are his towers – they often manage to combine in plan a circle and square (symbols of eternity and solidity) as they rise; are carved to represent trees ('. . . trees were the first temples'); are surmounted by domes to suggest the firmament, and in turn are topped by ringed finials '. . . to denote world soaring above world to the utmost empyrean' as in the pagoda Lethaby illustrates in the book. At the Horniman Museum there is a hint of the idea of the labyrinth in the complex 'Baroque' entrance, and circle and square are held together at the top of the tower by a girdle of the earth.

At the Passmore Edwards Settlement (1895) by Smith and Brewer, the very Richardsonian entrance, as found also in Townesend's work,[17] is capped by two eggs to symbolise creation. Such symbols had already occurred in the work of William Burges which Lethaby quotes with great approval.[18] H.W.Wilson's design for Ladbroke Grove Library (1890–1) was given an enormous Tree of Life climbing up the entire height of the façade. Also, his design for the extension of St Bartholomew's, Brighton (1898) treated the semi-dome of the apse as a 'ceiling like the sky' in a similar manner to Schultz Weir, as well as the apse in the collaborative design sent in under Wilson's name for the Liverpool Cathedral competition (1902).

Other examples may be waiting to be unearthed in the work of these and other architects. We may find that in examining the architecture of this period in terms of the Arts and Crafts movement, 'pioneers of the Modern Movement', and Edwardian architecture, we have overlooked those architects whose work could be more fruitfully read in the context of European Symbolism. Just as 'Queen Anne' had its icons, the sunflower and the peacock, so these architects had theirs, the Tree of Life – the most frequently used symbol, examples of which can also be seen in the work of Voysey and Frank Lloyd Wright. By far the most spectacular example must be the building ridiculed as 'The Golden Cabbage' – Joseph Olbrich's Vienna Secession Building (1897).

Olbrich, unusually for a Prix de Rome scholar, had spent part of his time in England in 1895. Not only this, but the influence of Charles Rennie Mackintosh may well have affected his work at this time. The link between Mackintosh and the Vienna Secessionists is well known. Not so well known is the fact that Mackintosh's first lecture, to the Glasgow Institute of Architects in February 1893, was an almost word for word copy of the Introduction from *Architecture, Mysticism, and Myth*.[19]

If we look for a building which satisfies all of Lethaby's conditions for a building to be a microcosm of the world we can do no better than the Watts Mortuary Chapel, Compton, Surrey, designed by Mary Watts (1896–1906). Before moving to Compton for the health of her husband, the Symbolist painter G.F.Watts, she had been a part of the attempt to bring art and handicraft to the workers of Whitechapel, where Townesend's sister was also involved.

In *A key to the symbols in the chapel at Compton* and the illustrated version of the guide *The Word in the Pattern* Mary Watts gave ample evidence of her intentions in the design of the chapel and one is hard put to do justice to the symbolism she there outlines. Central to her design philosophy was the desire '. . . to revive in some degree that living quality which was in all ornament when patterns had meaning'. Clearly then, like Lethaby, she saw contemporary design as devoid of meaning and sought to replace it by the use of mythic symbols.

The chapel itself, almost completely covered inside and out by symbolic decoration, was built by local people without professional assistance. The plan of the chapel employs a symbolism which Mary considered '... immeasurably older than any Celtic art – the Circle of Eternity, with the Cross of Faith running through it'. The effect of this combination inside the chapel is to suggest a large dome which becomes a 'world fabric', divided into four sections by openings, each section having its own '... Tree of Life, spreading its all embracing branches against the blue of heaven ... the whole woven, as it were, into a mystical garment'. Either side of the trees, after they have pushed themselves out of darkness and through '... a golden girdle, into which the emblems of the Trinity are wrought ...' stand '... winged messengers, alternately presenting the light or the dark side of all things ...' above him a '... Seraph clothed in the crimson colour of love and life' and at the top of the dome '... in token of the unthinkable Glory, is the circle of the Eternal – without begining, without end'.

Whether or not Mary knew of *Architecture, Mysticism, and Myth* we do not know. It has remained unjustifiably as ignored as has the chapel. Perhaps it does not really matter – both Lethaby and Mary Watts were seeking to put meaning back into architecture and design, to make it relevant to people's lives once again without resorting to historicism. Unfortunately their ideals were perhaps too impractical to appeal to architects of a revivalist persuasion. And in Lethaby's case they were irreconcilable with other ideals.

Both G.F.Watts and Lethaby knew and respected Edward Burne-Jones. He had been a convalescent at Little Holland House which, like Spiers house, was a central meeting place for the intellectuals and artists of the day.[21] G.F.Watts had painted symbolic schemes on its walls and dreamed up more imaginative ones (such as his gigantic 'House of Life' mural which was never executed) in the thirty years he stayed there as a guest. Burne-Jones had also provided a testimonial,[22] along with William Morris, for Lethaby's application to become Principal of the Central School of Arts and Crafts.

As students at the Royal Academy in 1883 Lethaby, Beresford-Pite and Attwood Slater shared a '... mutual admiration for Burne-Jones ...'[23] and sent in designs for the decorative painting prize. Although as students of the school of architecture their designs were not even considered, fifty years later Beresford-Pite was still of the opinion that '... if that design of Lethaby's could be unearthed now it would be a revelation to some of us of the meaning of progress of the decorative arts'.[24]

When one considers the above, plus the use Townesend made of murals in his designs, and the fact that the only contemporary architect Lethaby refers to in *Architecture, Mysticism, and Myth* is the very literary William Burges, one is presuaded that Lethaby had a strong desire for a narrative element in building which may well have come from Ruskin. For, if we are to take Lethaby's aphorisms seriously, one,[25] at least, points to this narrative element in his thinking about architecture – 'Architecture is building which is made to carry a story and convey a message'. Such a notion is clearly at variance with the honest building of Webb and also has little place in the theories of Modernism. While Webb may be said to have dominated Lethaby's practice it is evident that his wider theory came from Ruskin. By 1884, according to Schultz Weir, Lethaby had '. . . read everything that Ruskin had ever written and had absorbed his teaching'.[26] Lethaby too, at his 65th birthday celebration, spoke of '. . . the masters who have been prophets to me. The first was Ruskin . . .'

That Lethaby's clear desire for mystery was at variance with the clarity of story-telling does not seem to have bothered him. However, it bothered all of the reviewers of the book except the one for the Architectural Association. To employ symbols in the manner advocated for this '. . . art of the future . . .'[27] they would have to be intelligible, for as the reviewer for *The Builder* put it, '. . . it is but seldom . . . that architecture can rise entirely above utilitarian considerations and exist solely as an intellectual expression.'[28]

However, merely because symbolism is not immediately evident in a building does not mean it is not there. It is in its ability to act as a key to many more buildings than just those discussed here and as a major new approach to architectural theory in the later nineteenth century that Lethaby's book is so important.

NOTES

I am grateful to Peter Webb and Dr Mark Swenarton for many useful suggestions regarding clarity and fact respectively. The text is based on work in progress for a thesis at the Bartlett School of Architecture, University College London.

1 R.Blomfield. *RIBA Journal*, 20 Feb., 1932.
2 R.Schultz Weir. *AA Journal*, Vol. 73, June 1957.
3 R.Macleod *Style and Society* (1971).
4 For a subsequent attempt see William Stirling 'The Canon; an exposition of the pagan mystery perpetuated in the Cabala as the rule for all the arts' (1897).
5 A.R.N.Roberts *William Richard Lethaby; a volume in honour of the school's first principal* (1957).
6 The writer was E.W.Godwin.
  I am greatly indebted to Adrian Forty for this discussion of professionalism as outlined in his unpublished manuscript 'Problems in the history of a profession: Architecture in Britain in the Nineteenth and Twentieth Centuries'.
7 Ironically fed very much by *A,M,&M* as was the Free style.
8 *AA Notes*, Vol. 4, no. 32, Nov. 1889.
9 *A,M,&M*, p.XXI. (All page nos. refer to the 1974 edition).
10 *The Architect*, 22 January, 1892.
11 e.g. Samuel Bing's *Artistic Japan* (1888), De la Saussaye's *Manual of the Science of Religion* (1891), and J.G.Frazer's *The Golden Bough* (1891).
12 *The Times*, 31 Dec., 1891, p.4
13 *The British Architect*, Vol. 37, 8 Jan. 1892.
14 *AA Notes*, Vol. 7, 1891–2.
15 Illustrated in *The Builder*, 24 Nov. 1894.
16 Schultz Weir *ibid*.
17 Horace, brother of Charles Harrison Townesend, had met H.H.Richardson in Boston in the early 1880s, and he himself had visited England in 1882, including Spiers house. After this date his work began to receive much comment in the architectural press.
18 *A,A,&M*, p.254.
19 Introduction to *A,M,&M* by Godfrey Rubens, p.xvi–xvii.
20 Mary Watts, *A key to the symbols in the chapel at Compton* (1905), p.3.
21 For discussions of G.F.Watts and Holland House respectively see *England's Michaelangelo* by Wilfred Blunt and *Chronicles of Holland House 1820–1900* by G.S.H.F.Strangeways, 6th Earl of Illchester (1937).
22 Blomfield *ibid*.
23 Schultz Weir *ibid*.
24 Blomfield *ibid*.
25 Blomfield *ibid*. Lethaby used aphorisms '. . . for the support of his arguments and convictions, never for display'.
26 Schultz Weir *ibid*.
27 *A,M,&M*, p.8.
28 *The Builder*, Vol. LXII, 2 Jan, 1892.

Catalogue

Life

Lethaby's birthplace, mid nineteenth-century Barnstaple before the advent of the railway, was a typical English port and country town, which had hardly felt the effects of the Industrial Revolution. His father, a skilled carver and gilder, was typical of many radical Victorian craftsmen, hardworking, abstemious and devout and was undoubtedly an important influence on his son. Alexander Lauder, to whom the young William was apprenticed and where he stayed until he was twenty-one, was a designer of turgid Neogothic Methodist Chapels and, more significantly, an enthusiast for the decorative crafts, founding the Devon Art Pottery and a brick and terracotta works. Lethaby moved first to Derby, then to London and to the office of Norman Shaw as chief clerk. As apprentice and chief clerk he continued his brilliant student career, winning numerous competition prizes which enabled him to travel widely both in England and abroad. His rise had been rapid and he was to achieve an eminence in the architectural profession enjoyed by no other working-class boy in the nineteenth century.

Note:
All dimensions are given in centimetres

Early years

1
Shepherd, George
Barnstaple
Signed G.Shepherd. 1823
Watercolour over pencil (23 × 39)
Sutherland CII. 260.
Ashmolean Museum, Dept. of Western Art, Oxford.
Lethaby recalled: 'In the Bodleian library I found a delightful early watercolour view of my own town of Barnstaple, done in 1823, a kind little town seated in a smiling "landskip". There is something in these birthplaces and cradle homes which attack my very heart strings, and I never look at this town of mine from the outside without the "Jerusalem" feeling.'

2
Richard Pyle Lethaby (1824–1904)
Lethaby's father
Sepia photograph

3
2 Ebberley Lawn, Barnstaple
This was the family house where
W.R.Lethaby lived from 1860–1877.
Photographs, colour and black & white (GR)

4
St Anne's Grammar School, Barnstaple
Drawing by W.R.Lethaby
Pen and ink (60 × 40)
1870s

5
St Anne's Museum, Barnstaple
Colour photograph (GR)

1

6
Lauder, Alexander
The Methodist Chapel
Boutport Street, Barnstaple
Photographs (GR)

7
**Wesleyan Chapel, Cassland Road,
Homerton, London**
Designed by A.Lauder
Perspective drawing by W.R.Lethaby
reproduced in *The Architect*, Vol. 12 1874
p.18
Photograph (GR)

8
Chimneypiece
Designed and modelled by A.Lauder for
his own house 'Ravelin', Barnstaple;
probably made at Lauder & Smith's brick
and terracotta works, Barnstaple.
Photograph (GR)

9
Lauder, Alexander
Vase
Earthenware with leadglaze (23 × 14)
Made at the Devon Art Pottery, Barnstaple
which was founded by A.Lauder early in
the twentieth century.
Victoria and Albert Museum, Ceramic
Department

Lethaby the man

10
W.R.Lethaby as a young man
Two photographs in double frame
Private Coll.

11
Photographs of W.R.Lethaby
a. Lethaby in a boater
b. Lethaby at his desk
c. Lethaby with his dog 'Mr Brown' at 111
Inverness Terrace
d. Lethaby as a young man aged about 21
or 22 (the period he was appointed Norman
Shaw's Chief Clerk)
e. Cartoon of Lethaby from *Caricatures*
(London, 1926)

8

14

12
Calthorpe Street, WC1
Lethaby lived at 20 Calthorpe Street from
1880–1891.
Photograph (JM)

13
Letter on engagement of W.R.Lethaby
Letter of congratulation from Lady
Manners dated 10 May c.1900
Lady Constance Manners was the wife of
Lord Manners for whom Lethaby built
Avon Tyrrell, Hampshire.
Private Coll.

14
Edith Lethaby (née Rutgers Crosby)
Married Lethaby in 1901
a. Edith in the garden at 111 Inverness
Terrace with 2 pet dogs 'Solly' and
'Mr Brown'
b. Edith and Lethaby at Hartley Wintney
Photographs
Private Coll.

15
Inverness Terrace
Lethaby lived at 111 Inverness Terrace
from 1902 to his death.
a. Internal photographs 1932
b. External photographs c.1932

16
Johnston, Edward
Address to Professor W.R.Lethaby on
his retirement from the staff of the
Royal College of Art July 1919
Black and red pen on vellum (12 × 18)
Private Coll.
Written on the back in vermilion:
'Colophon Explanatory 1918–19 It is by the
Scribe's default that the Professor did not
get this letter a year ago (Alas! He who
shewed the Scribe a better way than "Art"
did not show him a longer way than
"Life".) Nevertheless, that it comes a year
late, may help to prove its authenticity –
besides indicating clearly the source of the
manuscript, it testifies to the fact that the
Professor is still warmly remembered by
the staff. E.J. script.
Sussex, July 1919 AD.'

17
Letter from W.R.Lethaby to the
Students of the Royal College of Art
dated 10 July 1919
Private Coll.
Letter of thanks from Lethaby on his
retirement from the Royal College.
The staff and students presented him with
a 'fine Bicycle . . . I find it most useful and
have named it "College".'

18
Rothenstein, W.
Drawing of W.R.Lethaby
c.1921
Photograph (GR)

19
Hartley Wintney (1918–1920)
a. Albion Cottage – Lethaby moved here
in 1918
b. Lethaby's grave
Photographs (GR)

Royal College of Art
South Kensington, London. August, 1918.
To Professor W. R. Lethaby from the Staff
of the Royal College of Art.

Dear Professor Lethaby,
Your retirement is a matter of great concern to us. We are truly sorry that you have to leave us and your loss makes us look forward with some anxiety to the future when we shall try to continue rightly the work so largely begun by You. But now we wish to thank you, and to bless you in return, for what you have done for us.
While innumerable difficulties and doubts must beset achievement – obstacles when a man is striving and uncertainties when he looks back & contemplates his work — we should like you to know and to be certain of this: that you have earned the respect and affection of every one of us and that you have strengthened our faith and courage.

In matters both of Faith and of Works you have always inspired us, and to know that you were with us helped to give us confidence in our own tasks and in each other. You cannot know how much you helped us – particularly by encouraging all our efforts to do good and real work (however feeble the worker's skill or its results). And besides this, all of us who have asked you for help have reason to remember some personal kindness on your part.
We hope that when you have left us you may not see the lessons you have taught us misapplied or perverted, but that you may see their fruition in works that at least come near achievement and aspire to goodness and reality.
July, 1919. We are, Yours sincerely,

16

20
Bayes, Gilbert RA
Bust of W.R.Lethaby
Bronze on short basal plinth
(60cm high)
Art-Workers' Guild

21
Letters to Sydney Cockerell on the
death of W.R.Lethaby
Private Coll.

22
Memorial inscription
Westminster Abbey.
Photograph (JM)

23
The Royal College of Art Lethaby
lectures
'W.R.Lethaby and his times': a series of six
lectures given by Basil Ward, Lethaby
Professor of Architecture.
Invitation cards
Held at the Lecture Theatre, Victoria &
Albert Museum, 1955–56.
In 1953 the Royal College of Art
established the Lethaby Chair of
Architecture.
This series of lectures was held to

commemorate the man who was for many
years Professor of Ornament and Design at
the Royal College of Art.
Numerous Lethaby Professors have
subsequently been appointed to lecture at
the Royal College of Art.

Student years

Debut designs
In 1877 *The Building News* started a
Designing Club with the object of
promoting the 'faculty of design'. At a time
when there was no properly organised
architectural education, the Club was to
become of some importance for young
architects. To qualify for the rather small
prize of £5 competitors had to submit at
least twelve designs. In January 1878 the
prize was won by W.R.Lethaby using the
pseudonym of 'Debut'.

24
Debut designs
Published in *The Building News* Vol. 32
1878–9
Extant collection containing 19 drawings in
pen and ink of which the following are
shown:
a. Mountain chapel (32 × 48)

b. Font, two views with section (36 × 45)
c. Wallpaper designs (35 × 24)
d. Temporary Chancel Screen 'Christmas decorations' (35 × 24)
e. Fender, coal scuttle and fire irons (35 × 24)
f. Dining room decoration (30 × 50)
g. Foliated hinges for a church door, with detail (35 × 24)
Private Coll.

25
Soane Medallion Award
1879
a. Royal Institute of British Architects Soane Medallion. Subjects for Medals and Prizes, 1878–79.
b. Soane Medallion Competition – reproduction in *The Building News*, 4 April 1879. 'A House for the Learned Societies' prize-winning design (Private Coll.) and details (reproduction) (Private Coll.)
c. Soane Medallion, St Anne's Museum, Barnstaple; ivory (5 cm diameter)
Lethaby commented on his design: 'The courtyard plan (adopted) would lend itself most readily to equality in arrangement of the four sets and to efficient lighting and privacy. The style chosen was the Renaissance, the chief intention of which was to do without an order and obtain some originality without the eccentricities of later developments.'

26
Royal Academy Schools
Ledger entry for W.R.Lethaby 6 July 1880
Lethaby attended the Royal Academy architecture classes as an evening student
Photograph (JM)

27
Pugin Studentship 1881
Lethaby's winning design
'Tomb of the Count de Borginival'
Reproduced in *The Building News* 9 Sep. 1881
Among the work that Lethaby submitted in 1881 for the Pugin Travelling Scholarship, was a measured drawing of the tomb of the Flemish Count de Borginival from a cast in the South Kensington Museum, subsequently published, which demonstrates his continuing interest in the northern Renaissance.

28
Pugin Travelling Studentship, 1881
An account of a tour in Somersetshire etc.
MS (210 × 340)
This account of his travels in the West Country was submitted as evidence of the work done during his tour.
British Architectural Library, RIBA, London

29
Design for St Anne's School, Streatham
Competition drawing
by W.R.Lethaby, M.E.Macartney and E.Newton 1882
Reproduction (original lost) from *The Architect* 25 November 1882
All that survives of this design is part of Lethaby's perspective for the centre of the main front. It shows a three-storey building of brick, stone and probably terracotta in a wild version of English Mannerism, tricked out with caryatids, scrolls, strapwork, enormous volutes and all manner of excesses (Private Coll.).

30
Tite Award Drawing
Royal Academy of Arts, Architectural School
1st Prize Design £25 Premium awarded to W.R.Lethaby
Design for a Bishop's Tomb
Pen and ink (51 × 68)
Private Coll.
The Building News, who published the drawing in 1882, said that it '... cribs from Waterhouse and Street ... In the style of the Earliest Decorated work, ... materials Purbeck marble for shafts, arches and mouldings, the carved parts being of soft stone wholly gilt, and the effigy of alabaster, painted and gilt.'

Lethaby's drawings, watercolours and sketchbooks

Arthur Keen, who worked with Lethaby in Norman Shaw's office, described Lethaby's prodigious activities as a draughtsman: 'Lethaby's output was enormous. I think I never knew a man who worked harder or to better effect; the evenings on which the Academy school was not open were commonly spent at the Kensington Museum, and to see Lethaby at work in a museum was to receive a useful lesson in close and exhaustive analysis. His power of observation is illustrated in everything he wrote, and he seemed able to refer confidently to things seen years before although studied at the time from quite a different standpoint. He was an untiring student and was continually making careful sketches. I remember that he had a useful habit of "collecting" particular details for a few weeks at a time; cast iron finials, for a time; then lettering; then perhaps lead pipe heads or wooden gates, and being on the look out for these things he found them everywhere. It is to be hoped that his drawings of every kind including Continental sketches and the drawings of the few buildings carried out by himself may be kept together and well indexed or grouped.'

31
Barnstaple: townscape
Pencil (35 × 26)
Athenaeum, Barnstaple

32
Huish Episcopi, Somerset
Signed by W.R.Lethaby. August 1888
Pencil (35 × 26)
Athenaeum, Barnstaple
Lethaby has written on this drawing in pen: 'The well known legend of Master and Apprentice is told of this Tower and that of Kingsbury Episcopi. In this case the Master killed himself and not the Apprentice. He is said to have jumped from his own tower.'

33
Capitals
5 drawings in pencil, one with red crayon
c.1883
Athenaeum, Barnstaple

34
Drawing of roof with decorated chimney and eaves
Pencil (35 x 26)
Unsigned
Central School of Art and Design

35

36a

35
Parthenon Frieze, British Museum
Detail
Pencil (17 × 25)
Athenaeum, Barnstaple

36
Drawings of lead work as used on fonts and vases
a. Font, Brookland, Kent. Pencil (22 × 14)
b. Vase, Hampton Court. Pencil (23 × 10)
Both of these illustrations were used in Lethaby's book *Leadwork* first published in 1893.
Athenaeum, Barnstaple

37
Mont St-Michel
Pencil drawing (25 × 18)
Signed W.R.L.
Athenaeum, Barnstaple

38
Townscape, probably in France showing circular tower
Watercolour and pencil (35 x 26)
Central School of Art and Design

39
Drawing of entrance to the Chrysotriclinium
1889
Pencil
Private Coll.
This imaginative reconstruction portrays the entrance to the Chrysotriclinium in the Imperial Palace of Constantine in Constantinople.

40
Plan for a road to run from the British Museum to Waterloo Bridge (unexecuted)
Signed W.R.Lethaby invent & delt.
(67 × 36)
Private Coll.

41
Scheme for Kingsway (unexecuted)
Charcoal and pencil (50 × 32)
Private Coll.

There are no catalogue entries 42 or 43

44
Path through a wood
Dated 1893
Pen and ink (46 × 44)
Signed W.R.Lethaby
Private Coll.

39

45
Sketchbook
1876–1879
Architectural details
Pencil (15 × 25)
British Architectural Library, RIBA, London

46
Sketchbook
1880
Drawings of chairs (18 × 12)
British Architectural Library, RIBA, London

47
Sketchbook
1880
A house at Rouen – all wood and carved all over
Black ink (17 × 12)
Athenaeum, Barnstaple

48
Sketchbook
1882
Architectural details
Pencil (19 × 12)
British Architectural Library, RIBA, London

49
Sketchbook
1883
Architectural details
Pencil (18 × 12)
British Architectural Library, RIBA, London

50
Sketchbook
1884
Architectural details
Pencil (18 × 11)
British Architectural Library, RIBA, London

51
Sketchbook
1885
Drawings of sculpture
Pencil (21 × 26)
British Architectural Library, RIBA, London

52
Sketchbooks
1887–1889
Pencil (20 × 16)
British Architectural Library, RIBA, London

53
Sketchbook
1898
Pencil (18 × 14)
Athenaeum, Barnstaple

54
Sketchbook
1905
Virgin and child
Watercolour (18 × 11)
British Architectural Library, RIBA, London

55
Sketchbook
1909
On the Danube, 19 August 1909
Pencil (18 × 11)
British Architectural Library, RIBA, London

56
Sketchbook
1912
Landscape
Watercolour (18 × 11)
British Architectural Library, RIBA, London
Alfred H.Powell, the ceramicist, recalled a sketching holiday spent in the company of Lethaby: 'I once went to Yorkshire with him on a holiday. You see these paintings on the walls; I tried to do something of the sort. He caught hold of my drawing and said, "Alfred, you don't know how to do it; you want to get lather into it", and he picked up a bunch of grass and, rubbing it over the drawing, produced a wonderful texture.'

Lethaby as architect and builder

Richard Norman Shaw appointed Lethaby his Chief Clerk in the summer of 1879. 'He was at the time twenty-two years of age', recalled Robert Schultz Weir, 'I have been told, by those that met him then, that he was shy and retiring and was at first over-awed by the presence of the great man into whose office he had come.' Within a short time Shaw trusted Lethaby to the extent of letting him design many of the decorative details of both the interior and exterior of his buildings which gave them, during the years that Lethaby worked for Shaw, their characteristic colour and texture. On 20 May 1889 Lethaby started his own practice at 9 Hart Street (now Bloomsbury Way) with a collection of small jobs which included work for Shaw. The break with his former Principal did not come until 1891 when he moved his office to Gray's Inn Square to be near to the man who became his hero – Philip Webb – of whom he said 'in his life I find a means of judging my own'. Most of Lethaby's few buildings were erected in the decade beginning in 1893 and each one was a complex and profound essay in invention on both imaginative and functional planes made manifest by fine workmanship. Whereas for Ruskin, Gothic was a style to be studied and emulated, Morris saw it more as a living popular tradition and organic building art. Inspired by Morris and Webb,

Lethaby along with other Arts and Crafts architects made structural experiments with modern materials. Lethaby was also deeply impressed by Morris's ideas on conservation and became actively involved with the Society for the Protection of Ancient Buildings and its struggle to save earlier buildings from destruction. As Surveyor of the Fabric at Westminster Abbey he was able to put these policies into practice so successfully that the anti-Scrape ideals of preservation rather than 'restoration' became widely accepted.

Norman Shaw years

57
Norman Shaw Memorial, New Scotland Yard
By W.R.Lethaby and H.Thornycroft
1914
Photograph (NBR)

57

58
St John the Baptist Church
Low Bentham, Yorkshire
Client: Mrs Alfred Foster
1876–78
a. Elevation of organ
Pencil on tracing paper, ink and wash
(53 × 61)
RA Norman Shaw Coll.
b. Pipe shades for organ full-size a, b and c.
Pen and wash (65 × 50)
RA Norman Shaw Coll.
c. Photograph

59
Armchair
Designed by either R.N.Shaw or
W.R.Lethaby
c.1876/1880
Turned oak (115 × 55 × 49)
V&A Dept. of Furniture and Woodwork
Chair in the Queen Anne style designed for
the Tabard Inn, Bedford Park

Fleet, Devonshire
Shortly after Lethaby went to Bloomsbury
Square, Shaw fell ill and the responsibility
for much of the design of this
reconstruction was delegated to Lethaby.
This was his first major architectural
project.

60
Fleet, Devonshire
Client: Henry Bingham Mildmay
Reconstruction of house by stages, and new
wing
1878–1883
a. Elevation and section of steps in billiard
room
Pen and wash on tracing paper (40 × 55)
RA Norman Shaw Coll.
b. Plan of steps in billiard room
Pen and wash on tracing paper
RA Norman Shaw Coll.
c. Elevation of organ in saloon
Signed: N.Shaw 20.9.1883
Pen and wash on tracing paper
RA Norman Shaw Coll.

61
**St James's Branch Offices of the
Alliance British and Foreign Life and
Fire Assurance Company of
Bartholomew Lane**
1881–1883
Designed by R.Norman Shaw with
drawings by W.R.Lethaby and details
designed by Lethaby
Reproduction in *The Building News* 26
May 1882
'It is', wrote Arthur Keen, a clerk of
Shaw's, 'one of the most fully detailed
buildings in London and remarkable for the
way in which richness is secured without
loss of breadth. Lethaby made most of the
drawings for it but the first drawing of it
was made by Shaw.' Lethaby was also
responsible for designing many of the
details.
Private Coll.

62
Cragside, Rothbury, Northumberland
Client: Sir William Armstrong
Designs for interior
1883
a. Fireplace.
Finished perspective of chimney piece
Signed: W.R.Lethaby
Pen (46 × 54)
RA Norman Shaw Coll.
b. Fireplace.
Details of strapwork and putti
Pencil (64 × 50)
RA Norman Shaw Coll.
c. Tracings of fireplace
RA Norman Shaw Coll.
d. Lock case, full-size drawing
Pencil (36 × 20)
RA Norman Shaw Coll.
e. Photographs
The fireplace was Italian marble, by
Farmer and Brindley, one of the most
successful Victorian marble masons. The
mixture of early English and French
Renaissance motifs is characteristic of
Lethaby's designs of this period. To quote
Andrew Saint: 'The chimneypiece,
dwarfing all other fittings, imbues the
atmosphere with a grand sensuality, as if
the change from Old English to
Renaissance, from darkness to light, has let
loose from restraint a current of opulence,
self-indulgence and physicality'.

63
Port Elizabeth, All Saints' Church
Unexecuted project
c.1885
Perspective
Signed: W.R.Lethaby
Pen and ink (96 × 61)
RA Norman Shaw Coll.
An unexecuted project for a mission church
in Africa which probably influenced the
Australian architect Robin Dodd in his
work at Brisbane. The startling deep
window embrasures were obviously
designed for a hot climate.

64
Holy Trinity Church, Latimer Road
1887
a. Design for organ: perspective
Insc.: Design for organ, Holy Trinity,
Latimer Road, W (To be printed in neat
lettering in centre)
Signed and dated: R.Norman Shaw RA
July 1887
Pen (430 × 290 approx.)
British Architectural Library, RIBA,
London
b. East elevation
Pen and wash on mounted tracing paper
(39 × 52)
RA Norman Shaw Coll.
c. Photograph of interior of church from
The Architect, 25 October 1889
(36 × 45)
RA Norman Shaw Coll.
Although the idea and development of the
church was Shaw's, all the details, font,
organ, stalls, pulpit, window tracery and
reredos were brilliantly designed by
Lethaby. All but the last are now
destroyed.

Lethaby's Buildings

65
**Avon Tyrrell, near Ringwood,
Christchurch, Hants**
1891–1893
Client: Lord Manners
a. Contract drawings for the house and
offices.
Basement and ground-floor plans and
section.
East and west elevations, elevation and end
elevation of outbuildings and section of
outbuildings

Pen and coloured washes with some blue crayon (475 × 685)
British Architectural Library, RIBA, London
b. Revised (?) contract drawings for the house.
North (entrance) elevation
Pen, blue wash and red crayon on linen-backed tracing paper (425 × 725)
May 1891
British Architectural Library, RIBA, London
c. Garden elevation
Insc.: Garden room not in contract
Pen, blue wash and red crayon on linen-backed tracing paper (425 × 725)
British Architectural Library, RIBA, London
d. Contract drawing
Pen and pencil with coloured washes (510 × 690)
British Architectural Library, RIBA, London
e. Photographs (JL)

Two external views and the drawing room at Avon Tyrrell

f. Designs for table
i. sketch of table seen from above, pen and ink
ii. 1/12 scale working drawing, ink and pencil
This large country house, built for Lord and Lady Manners, was Lethaby's first independent commission and its design owes much to both Shaw and Webb. The simplicity of the building is more apparent than real, for the design of a number of its features owes much to aesthetic rather than purely functional considerations. Several of the details, such as the peacocks either side of the chimney stack which were the emblem of the Manners family, relate to the symbolism elaborated by Lethaby in his *Architecture, Mysticism, and Myth* of 1891.

66
The Hurst, Hartopp Road, Four Oaks Park, Sutton Coldfield, Warwickshire
New House and Stables
Client: Charles Edward Mathews
1892
a. First-floor plan
Verso: sketch of Venetian-type window for north elevation
Pen and coloured washes (515 × 680)
British Architectural Library, RIBA, London
b. East and south elevations, to the former of which is added in pencil a single-bay addition
Pen and coloured washes (685 × 510)
British Architectural Library, RIBA, London

c. North and west elevations and sections E.E and F.F
Verso: sketch details of windows of S and E elevations
Pen and coloured washes (680 × 510)
British Architectural Library, RIBA, London
d. Photographs (GR)
The Hurst was built for Charles Edward Mathews and exemplifies what Lethaby meant by 'Expressionist forms [which] express the shape of the spaces within but this expression also serves to signal their function'.

Views of The Hurst, including the stables (bottom)

67
Melsetter House, Hoy, Orkney Islands
Client: Thomas Middlemore
Extensive alterations, additions and estate works
1898
Lethaby converted a former laird's house and a group of outbuildings into a medium-sized country house for Thomas Middlemore, a successful Birmingham industrialist. The largest single work was the sensitive transformation of the old house, steading and a miscellany of outbuildings into an informal, but coherently organised country house. As far as possible the old buildings were preserved.
a. Plans and elevations of Melsetter by John Brandon-Jones
Private Coll.
b. Photographs of the house before 1898
Private Coll.
c. Photographs (GR and JL)

Furniture by W.R.Lethaby for Melsetter House
Dresser
Unpolished oak inlaid with ebony, sycamore and bleached mahogany
Designed by W.R.Lethaby in 1900 for Melsetter House, Hoy, Orkney Islands.
V&A Department of Furniture
d. Photograph
e. Design for inlay, pen and ink, pencil full-size (44 × 54)
Private Coll.
f. Table
Designed by W.R.Lethaby, executed by Mason.
c.1900
Light wood with ebony inlay
(46 × 100 × 71)
Private Coll.

Chapel of SS. Colm and Margaret
Melsetter, Hoy, Orkney Islands
1900
In this design Lethaby sought to express something that was characteristic of the wayside chapels of the North – more powerful and more primitive than the quiet

domesticity of Melsetter House. Easily distinguishable from the other buildings on the estate in its construction of massive random rubble and roughly dressed quoins, it was innocent of harling and roofed, like the house, with large Caithness stone slates. The interior, as built, is both simpler and more personal than Lethaby's first designs for the chapel, for the vault which rises from low walls has been formed of mass concrete over shuttering, and a single arch bridges the nave, separating it from the chancel.

g. First design for chapel
1900
Ink on tracing paper
Private Coll.

h. Second and executed design for chapel
1900
Ink on tracing paper
Private Coll.
Photographs (GR and DL)

i. Rysa Lodge, Hoy, Orkneys
Watercolour (25 × 35)
by John Brandon-Jones. Private Coll.
This watercolour illustrates Rysa Lodge (the hunting lodge of the Melsetter Estate) which Lethaby had converted from a croft c.1899.

Opposite and above:
Melsetter House, with the dresser in
unpolished oak inlaid with ebony, sycamore
and bleached mahogany, which was
designed by Lethaby

68
High Coxlease, Lyndhurst, Hampshire
Client: Thomas Eustace Smith
New House and stables
1901
Photographs (GR and JL)
Drawing reconstruction of ground floor and
first floor (GR)

A medium-sized country house designed
for Eustace Smith who was seeking
seclusion in the New Forest almost twenty
years after his involvement in the notorious
Sir Charles Dilke divorce case in which
both Smith's wife and daughter were cited.
The regularity of the design is broken by
variations in the roof heights and the tall
chimney stacks which were made necessary
by the surrounding trees.

Above and right: High Coxlease,
Lyndhurst.
Opposite: All Saints, Brockhampton

69
**Church of All Saints, Brockhampton,
Ross-on-Wye, Herefordshire
New memorial church**
Client: Alice Foster
Designed 1901, built 1902
a. 2 original photos showing building in
progress (Private Coll.)
b. Contract drawing
North and south elevations, east and west
ends and section through chancel etc.
Insc.: Stamped E.C.E./630345/25 Apr
1901
Pencil with grey, grey-green and sepia
washes, alterations in red pen
British Architectural Library, RIBA,
London
c. Section of nave, an alternate section of
transepts and section of arch stone
Insc.: As above and includes some
measurements and notes on method of
construction dated May 28, 1901
Pencil and pen with green, grey and yellow
washes on linen-backed tracing paper
British Architectural Library, RIBA,
London

d. Detail of windows showing plans and
elevations of inside of west, east and nave
windows and elevations of two light
windows in side walls of chancel and of
belfry lights
Pencil, pen, blue crayon and buff wash on
cartridge backed with tracing paper
Signed: W.R.Lethaby Architect 2 Gray's
Inn Square WC
British Architectural Library, RIBA, London
e. Typescript of the *Specification of
Materials/to be used and works to be done
in/building a Memorial Church at/
Brockhampton in the County of Hereford
from the Plans and under the
Superintendance of Mr W.R.Lethaby of 2/
Gray's Inn Square London. Architect* (the
address crossed out and replaced in red pen
by *111 Inverness Terrace, W.*); the
specification is dated April 1901)
11 pages (330 × 200)
British Architectural Library, RIBA,
London
f. Cartoon for stained glass by Christopher
Whall
Left-hand light of the west window
St Margaret of Scotland visiting the sick
1909
Charcoal (137 × 42)
William Morris Gallery, Walthamstow
g. Sketch design by Christopher Whall
East window
Christ in Majesty, Saints and Angels
1902
Watercolour, ink and pencil (37 × 21)
William Morris Gallery, Walthamstow
h. Sketch design by Christopher Whall
West window
Saints
1909
Watercolour, ink and pencil (20 × 12)
William Morris Gallery, Walthamstow
i. Sketch design by Christopher Whall
South transept
Four angels
1916
Watercolour, ink and pencil (38 × 20)
William Morris Gallery, Walthamstow
j. Photographs (GR and JL)
The typed instructions exhibited here are
the specifications which formed part of the
contract between Lethaby and his
American client, Alice Madeline Foster.
Mrs Foster had commissioned the church
in memory of her American parents, the

Jordans, founders of the firm Jordan,
Marsh and Co. Lethaby dispensed with the
technical skills of a building contractor and
the church was built by direct labour, with
Lethaby assuming full responsibility for
construction and materials. The church was
originally intended to have a conventional
cover but in the short period between the
approval of the contract drawings and the
final specification of materials the decision
was taken to use mass concrete formed over
'rough boards' and thatch. Undoubtedly
the work on the chapel at Melsetter,
completed less than a year before, had
given Lethaby the confidence and
experience needed for this far more
ambitious scheme. Randell Wells acted as
Clerk of the Works while Lethaby remained

70

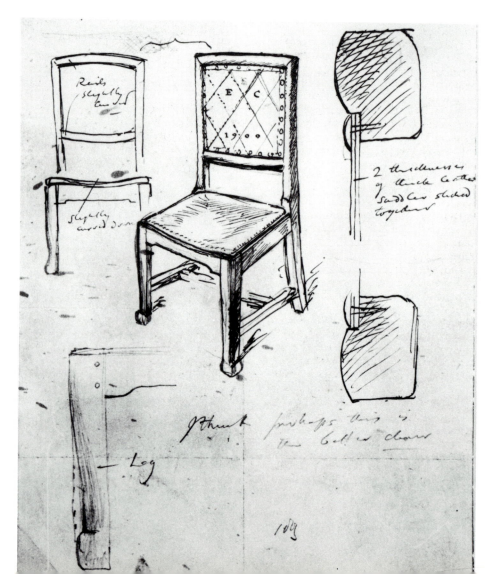

in London; but this resulted in certain difficulties: 'then ... I came in one morning to find him [Lethaby] all upset again, this time because he had just discovered that Mr Wells had made the tower eight or ten feet higher than the original plan! and so it went on'. In the end actual costs exceeded the initial estimate, much to the annoyance of Mrs Foster.

70
Eagle Insurance Buildings, Colmore Row, Birmingham, Warwickshire
New Offices 1900
Client: Eagle Insurance Co. Ltd.
a. Plans and elevation by John Brandon-Jones.
Private Coll.
b. Photograph from Muthesius' *Die Englische Baukunst der Gegenwart* (1900) showing the façade before the removal of the inscriptions
c. Front elevation and back elevation (the latter showing suggested incorporation of letters EIC at the top of the building)
Signed: W.R.Lethaby and J.L.Ball Architects
Verso: Sketch detail for plaque over the entrance door with the date 1899 revised to 1900
Insc.: As above, labelled and with pencil notes and amendments
Pen and coloured washes (535 × 730)
British Architectural Library, RIBA, London
d. Drawing, design for chair in Eagle Insurance building
Pen and ink (27 × 21)
Private Coll.
e. Photographs (GR, JL, JB-J)
This office block stands on an important street in the centre of Birmingham. The right-hand door gave access to the insurance company's offices on the ground floor and the one on the left to a variety of different offices intended for independent letting on the floors above. Although the subject of debate in the past, there can be little doubt that the building was designed by Lethaby and carried out by J.Ball from his Birmingham office. There is a sharp contrast between the modern materials used in the construction (such as concrete and metal joists) and the esoteric iconography of the façade. Lethaby was also responsible for the design of numerous interior details.

71

Project for Liverpool Cathedral

71
Liverpool Cathedral competition project
Designed by W.R.Lethaby, H.Wilson, R.W.S.Weir, H.Ricardo, F.Troup, Stirling Lee and C.Whall
1902
a. Montage. Photo of cemetery and drawing
b. Montage. Photo of cemetery and drawing
c. Section towards altar
d. Plan at floor level
e. Decoration of ceiling
f. Three photos of model
g. Eastern apse
h. West end
Photographs from drawings in V&A Dept. of Prints and Drawings (JM)
i. Sketch design

Pen and ink (41 × 26)
Private Coll.
j. Photograph of Cathedral today (NBR)
The 1902 competition for the design of the Cathedral produced many entries including this most unconventional design. The project was submitted by Lethaby (who was responsible for the structural idea), Henry Wilson, Halsey Ricardo, F.W.Troup, Stirling Lee, Chris Whall and R.Schultz Weir. The building specifications have been lost but it seems most probable that it was to be constructed in mass concrete. The building gives visible expression to some of Lethaby's ideas on the use of concrete: 'Concrete gives the possibility of erecting solid roofs. Such a system of homogeneous building with roofs of cylindrical, conical, domical or other forms ... opens up large possibilities of more dignified and interesting types of

72

planning as well as more monumental superstructures . . . In concrete fabrics – the naked and unashamed show energy and experimental thinking.' It is the use of mass concrete which would explain the corrugations and spherical triangles of the self-buttressing design which are a product of structural necessity and not only the result of an attempt at Byzantine revival.

Symbolism

Lethaby's first book *Architecture, Mysticism, and Myth* (1891) advanced the notion that philosophical and theological ideas were symbolically expressed in the forms and decorations of ancient architecture. Despite its unscholarly nature it provided some badly needed profundity in contemporary architectural thinking and many of the symbolic forms and ideas that were discussed were taken up and used by those young architects and designers who were trying to develop a style free of Gothic or classical influences. For a while

Lethaby's researches for the book provided him with material for new ideas but he soon came to understand that one of the tasks of the modern architect was to evolve a readily intelligible symbolism which would be the expression of scientific ideas such as function and construction.

72
Frontispiece and title-page of
Architecture, Mysticism, and Myth
Among those who drew inspiration from this book were May Morris, R. Schultz Weir, Mary Watts in the Watts mortuary chapel, Henry Wilson and C. R. Mackintosh in a lecture titled 'Architecture' given before the Glasgow Institute of Architects. This lecture, which Mackintosh's biographer, Professor Howard, has described as an intellectual achievement of some importance, was taken, without acknowledgement, almost word for word from Lethaby's introduction.

73
Frontispiece and Title Page
Architecture, Nature and Magic
In this excellent study of the sources of certain architectural and decorative forms, Lethaby describes his previous study, *Architecture, Mysticism, and Myth* as 'very insufficient and in many ways feeble second-rate and second-hand authorities were mixed up with true sources, and the whole thing uncritical and inexpert.'
Published in parts in *The Builder*, 1928
By Duckworth & Co. 1956

Influence of the *Hypnerotomachia Poliphili*
74
Colonna, Francesco
Hypnerotomachia Poliphili, VBI Humana Omnia Non Nisi Somnium Esse Ostendit, At Qve Obiter Plurima Scitv Sanequam Digna Commemorat.
Venice, Aldus 1499
Methuen Facsimile 1904
(33 × 21)
Central School Coll.

The *Hypnerotomachia* had a profound impact on literature, art and printing. The story is an allegorical romance concerning the dream of Poliphilus in which he travels

through classical landscapes in search of his beloved. Classical objects and architectural details appear both in the numerous illustrations and interspersed throughout the text. The text, printed in roman letters, was much admired and influential on subsequent publications. The book is a unique record of fifteenth-century Italian knowledge of art and architecture of the classical revival.

75
Architectural Association Sketchbook 1899
Frontispiece by W. R. Lethaby
This decoration was inspired by the *Hypnerotomachia*; the lower design shows a world temple at the centre of a labyrinth.

75

79

76
A Garden Enclosed
Photograph of drawing
By W.R.Lethaby
An illustration to J.Sedding's *Gardens Old and New*. Lethaby's description (published in 1923) was an indirect attack on the practices of his contemporaries' period designs (and his own earlier interest in Symbolism): 'Period-style Jacobean.... As this design belongs to the joyous period of the opening Renaissance we might venture to scratch a sonnet on the pillar ... On sunny summer days a velvet doublet and a rapier would look well at the base of the column under the sonnet.'
V&A Dept. of Prints and Drawings

77
Design for a chair, the 'Throne of London'
By W.R.Lethaby
Illustration, The Art-Workers' Guild Mask performed June 27, 28, 29 & 30 1899
Designed in 1899 for the Art-Workers' Guild Mask 'Beauty's Awakening'. In an attack twenty-three years later on designing in period styles, Lethaby used a version of this design and his own drawing 'A Garden Enclosed' as examples of what he, by then, considered sham art. His ironical description of the throne and its making reads:
'Period-style, early Byzantine. A Bishop's chair of gilt silver and ivory, Alexandrian manner, about AD 490. To be framed up in cypress or cedar and covered with plate-silver as shown; crystal balls on the arms. The decorations are a series of carved ivory tablets, which must be executed from full-size details ... The ivories will have to be baked at the completion of the work to yellow the colour and mellow the tone; slight cracks are to be produced, but not too many, and the gilding is to be partly rubbed off.'

Sun symbols
78
Eagle Insurance Buildings, Colmore Row, Birmingham, Warwickshire
W.R.Lethaby
Photograph of façade before alteration
From Muthesius' *Die Englische Baukunst der Gegenwart* (1900)

79
Illustration of the Sun Temple at Baalbek
R. Wood and James Dawkins' *The Temples of Palmyra and Baalbeck* (1753)
'In the classic period of Syrian art most of the great temple doors had sculptured on the under side of the epistyle an enormous eagle with expanded wings. The great eastern door of the sun temple at Baalbek, "city of the sun", is the finest of these; it is 21 feet wide, and therefore, some 40 feet high ...'
'The lintel of Palmyra is figured by Wood and Dawkins. The door faces due east, and the great eagle appears to fly into the temple, the wings expanded ten or twelve feet; the rest of the space is occupied by stars, and two genii of the dawn.'

80
Illustration, Buddhist gateway
From *Architecture, Mysticism, and Myth*
Lethaby's illustration of a great Buddhist gateway with triple lintels and sun discs was the source for the design of the two doorways of the Sun Eagle Insurance Buildings.

81
Sun Eagle Insurance Buildings, Colmore Row, Birmingham
First design
W.R.Lethaby
In an attempt to provide a unifying theme divorced from designing in the styles, Lethaby hit on the idea of using symbols, such as crested eagles derived from sun temples as decorative motifs. This early design shows two such birds which were, however, deleted in the final design.

82
Eagle Insurance Buildings
W.R.Lethaby
Colour photograph (JL)

83
Drawing for illustration
From *Architecture, Mysticism, and Myth*
by W.R.Lethaby
Private Coll.
Lethaby's illustration of a tomb at Shefa Amr in Galilee which figures a sun disc on the arch. 'It was this tradition that was

80

afterwards followed in the universal Syrian Christian custom of placing a disc with the sacred monogram or cross on the lintel, usually with ribbon-like appendages, right and left, which are direct survivals of the Egyptian uraeus, that in a similar position accompanied the sun's orb. This becomes a decorative commonplace in Byzantine art, either at Constantinople or Venice.'

Four square symbols
84
The Bell Tower, All Saints, Brockhampton 1902
W.R.Lethaby
Photograph (GR)
The bell tower consists of a pyramid superimposed on two cubes. 'Of all forms', wrote Lethaby, 'the cube and the hemisphere are the most sacred; the first was that of the Sanctuary at Jerusalem, and that chosen by St John as the type of the Holy city ...'

'This four squareness was a talismanic assurance of permanence and stability. The thought that, as the heavens were stable upon the earth, so any building four square with them would be immovable, seems, as we have seen, a natural analogy.'

85
The Horniman Museum, London Road, Forest Hill, Lewisham, South London (1896–1901)
C.Harrison Townesend
Photograph
'. . . the magical combinations of square with circle (universe with Earth), cube with hemisphere, tree with stone, were expressed even more clearly in the tower of the Horniman Museum . . .'. The mosaic panel is by Robert Anning Bell, a member of the Art-Workers' Guild.

The World Temple
86
Bellcote, Avon Tyrrell
W.R.Lethaby 1891
Photograph (GR)
Drawing (GR)
This small structure can be seen to relate to Lethaby's ideas on buildings as microcosms. In *Architecture, Mysticism, and Myth* he speaks of 'a local reduplication of the . . . World Temple itself – a sort of model to scale, its form governed by the science of the time . . . its place was exactly below the celestial prototype; like that it was sacred, like that it was strong, its foundations could not be moved, if they were placed foursquare to the walls of the firmament'.

87
Chalice
Designed and made by H.Wilson with the assistance of S.Wiseman and H.G.Murphy
Silver, parcel gilt decorated with enamel, niello and semi-precious stones. London, c.1900
27 cm high
Gloucester Cathedral Treasury
The Victoria and Albert Museum *Victorian Church Art* catalogue describes the chalice:
'The knot formed as the Temple of the Lamb, with four arched openings supported by pillars of rock crystal, surmounted by pediments bordered with

85

rope moulding and with pinnacles between; embellished with enamel and semi-precious stones. The Lamb is silver-gilt, on a mountain from which run the Four Rivers of Paradise, Pison, Gihon, Hiddekel and Euphrates. The foot embattled with seven domes, seven trees and seven towers, set with fire opals; arcaded base.' The circular stem is decorated with wavy patterns in niello.
Henry Wilson, architect and designer and close friend of Lethaby's, seems to have drawn frequently on *Architecture, Mysticism, and Myth* for inspiration in his own work. The complex imagery of Wilson's chalice relates to several passages of Lethaby's book; in describing the perfect temple Lethaby speaks of: 'the four square enclosure on the top of the world mountain, where the polar tree or column stands, and whence issue the four rivers. From the thought of such an enclosure we get . . . our word Paradise.' The sacred number seven appears in the account of the heavenly mountain of the gods: 'It ascends by seven spurs on which the seven separate cities and palaces of the gods are built, amid green woods and murmuring streams, in seven circles placed one above the other.'

This world mountain relates to the 'tradition of the throne on seven heavenly steps [which] lasts on into the Middle Ages'.

88
Design for the base of a chalice
By H.Wilson
Feb. 20, 1898/9
V&A Dept. of Prints and Drawings
Photograph (GR)

The Sky and Heavens
89
Liverpool Cathedral Project, Apse Semidome
W.R.Lethaby
Watercolour
Photograph (GR)
'It may be said that at great periods of architecture ceilings were always skies. Viollet-le-Duc tells us, in his *Dictionnaire de l'Architecture* (Art. Peinture), that the whole scheme of interior colour had to be readjusted in the thirteenth century to harmonise with the vaults, which were painted the most brilliant of blues, *parsemee*, with gold stars, against which nothing could hold its own but vermilion, black and more gold.'

The Hearth
90
Navel stone and two flanking birds
Illustration from *Architecture, Mysticism, and Myth*
Photograph (GR)
The arrangement of chimney and stack and attendant peacocks (the Manners emblem) made Avon Tyrrell symbolically the hub and navel of the Manners family. The idea is derived from Lethaby's drawing of the Centre Stone at Delphi which had two eagles placed at its sides and marked the sacred centre or omphalos of the earth. Furthermore the hearth was identified with the navel or focus of the house and hence of the family.

91
Avon Tyrrell
Exterior chimney
W.R.Lethaby
Photograph

Tree of Life
92
Watts Mortuary Chapel, Compton, Surrey
Photograph (JM)
Designed by Mary Watts in 1896, the memorial chapel is embellished with numerous symbolic forms, some of which (the Tree of Life, the Labyrinth, e.g.) may come directly from Lethaby's *Architecture, Mysticism, and Myth*.

93
The Bishopsgate Institute, Bishopsgate, City of London
C.Harrison Townesend
1892–94
Photograph (JM)
Harrison Townesend's design for the Institute won a competition in 1892. The building consists of a large library and public hall. As pointed out by Alastair Service: 'In the highly original frontage can be seen a free adaptation of Elizabethan architecture, as well as the influence of H.H.Richardson and Henry Wilson. On the walls of the building is the tree of life symbol, sculptured with branches flowing over the surface, contrasting with other areas of plain masonry. Such a surface treatment of the motif might have seemed entirely beside the point to Lethaby himself, but that does not alter the likelihood that it was done under the influence of his writings.'

94
Façade, Whitechapel Art Gallery 1899–1901
C.Harrison Townesend
Photograph (GR)
Shortly after *Architecture, Mysticism, and Myth* was published, Harrison Townsend started integrating symbolic nature into the façade of his buildings.

Pavements like the Sea
95
Pavement
Westminster Cathedral c.1912
By Robert Schultz Weir
a. Watercolour (39 × 46)
Private Coll.
b. Chapel as executed: Photograph (JM)
c. Portrait of R.W.S.Weir: Photograph
Schultz Weir paid tribute to the impact of *Architecture, Mysticism, and Myth* recalling how the book had 'opened up to us younger men a hitherto undreamed of, romance in architecture. The labyrinth, the Golden Gates of the Sun, pavements like the Sea . . . now through Lethaby one began to understand something of what they all meant. I was at that time about to do a small private chapel, into it went a pavement like the sea and ceiling like the sky, as an accepted tradition.' Schultz Weir is, however, probably referring to another chapel and not the one illustrated here.

95c

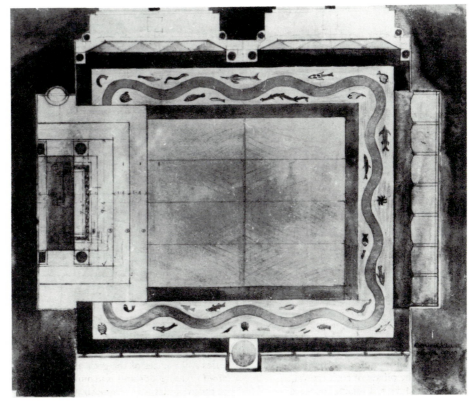

95a

Symbols of Creation
96
Mary Ward Centre
9 Tavistock Place, London WC1
Designed by Smith and Brewer
Photograph (JM)
Dunbar Smith and Cecil Brewer produced
the winning designs for a competition for
the Passmore Edwards Settlement (later
known as the Mary Ward Settlement), a
large charitable building in Tavistock
Place. The prominent stone doorway is
topped by two enormous eggs, undoubtedly
an allusion to Lethaby's belief that 'the egg
is the typical germ and therefore the natural
symbol of creation'. Lethaby was to design
a fireplace for the building.

Symbols from Poetry
97
A Beryl Shrine
By W.R.Lethaby
Illustrated in *The Architect* 20 Jan. 1888
Contemporary poetry was another source of
inspiration for Lethaby. His drawing 'The
Beryl Shrine' may have been inspired by
Joseph Knight who in his *Life of Rossetti*
(1887) wrote of the poem *Rose Mary*: 'The
picture of Rose Mary passing by the secret
path her feet had not trodden before, to the
altar, and her destruction of the beryl,
would supply a fine subject for a painting
...' The passage reads:

'The altar stood from its curved recess
In coiled serpent's life like-ness:
Even such a serpent evermore
Lies asleep at the world's dark core
Till the last Voice shakes the sea and shore.

From the altar-cloth a book rose spread
And tapers burned at the altar head:
And there in the altar-midst alone
Twixt wings of sculptured beast unknown
Rose Mary saw the Beryl-stone.'

The serpent originated in a sketch Lethaby
did to illustrate some lines of Keats' 'Lancia':

'A palpitating snake
Bright and cirque
Couchant in a dusky brake
She was a gordian shape of dazzling line
Sprinkled with stars like Ariadne's tears.'

97

Lethaby and Westminster Abbey

Lethaby was Surveyor to the Fabric of
Westminster Abbey from 1906 until 1927.
In place of the previous policies of
restoration where parts of the building were
reinvented in neo-Gothic styles by Pearson
and Scott, Lethaby substituted a policy of
mending and cleaning – a kind of building
dentistry – which resulted in the
rediscovery of many treasures including
medieval carvings and wall paintings. He
succeeded in preserving those parts of the
fabric which had been due for demolition at
the time of his appointment.

98
**Photograph at Westminster Abbey of
W.R.Lethaby, Dean Armitage
Robinson and E.J.Scott, Keeper of the
Muniments.**
Pre-1911
Photograph (Benjamin Stone)
By courtesy of the Dean & Chapter of
Westminster

99
Photograph of W.R.Lethaby
In the uniform of the Surveyor of
Westminster Abbey which he wore for the
Coronation of George V in 1911.
Private Coll.

100
**Letter from W.R.Lethaby on his
appointment to Westminster Abbey, to
Thackeray Turner**
SPAB

101
Westminster Abbey today
Photographs
a. Exterior (NBR)
b. Cloister (JM)

102
Westminster Abbey
Photographs
a. West end
b. Cloisters
c. North Porch
d. South Transept, 1860 before
'Restoration'
SPAB

103
Westminster Abbey Re-examined
By W.R.Lethaby
Duckworth 1925
L.Tanner's copy
Letter from Lethaby tipped in
By courtesy of the Dean & Chapter of
Westminster
Lethaby's book *Westminster Abbey Re-
examined* (1925) broke entirely new
ground; Lawrence Tanner, sometime
Keeper of the Muniments, wrote that it was
'the foundation upon which almost all
subsequent research on Mediaeval
craftsmen has been based'.

104
'Reynder', Chapter House wall painting
Watercolour (330 × 250) by W.R.Lethaby
By courtesy of the Dean & Chapter of
Westminster

105
**Pattern of gold work outside the arms
of the Coronation chair**
Pencil and wash (250 × 350) by
W.R.Lethaby
By courtesy of the Dean & Chapter of
Westminster

Lethaby and the the Society for the Protection of Ancient Buildings

Lethaby was introduced to SPAB by
Gimson in 1891; he became a Committee
member in 1893. He undertook numerous
enquiries and was involved in compiling
many reports. He became a leader in the
constellation of architects grouped round
Webb. A scholarship introduced by the
Society in 1930 was named after Lethaby.
'It was Gimson who introduced me to the
Society and the circle in 1891. For a time –
a great time for me – we attended the
meetings from 5–7, and then went across
the Strand to Gatti's for an evening meal:
Morris often, Webb always, and two or
three of a number of younger lesser people,
Gimson, Emery Walker, Sydney Cockerell
. . . and myself.'

106
Rochester Cathedral
Letter from W.R.Lethaby to Mr Powys of
SPAB on the proposed repair to Gandulf's
tower, Rochester Cathedral.
11.11.1922
(200 × 255)
SPAB
Photograph

107
A School of Rational Builders
Exhibition catalogue
1983
SPAB

Lethaby as designer

At the turn of the century much of an
architect's time was taken up with the
design of ornament in one or more of the
historicist styles and Lethaby was no
exception. His early decorative work
especially for Shaw is very fine but soon in
an attempt to deepen the content of his
work outside the clichés of historicist styles
he turned to other sources like the
Hypnerotomachia for inspiration. This was
but an interlude to be followed by the
designs for Kenton and Company which set
the pattern for the rest of his career. Here
the decorative effects are of extreme
simplicity achieved through the
manipulation of colour and texture. This
rejection of historicism and the
preoccupation with truth to materials
manifest the ideals of the Arts and Crafts
Exhibition Society which Lethaby helped
to found.

Designs for metalwork

The earliest of Lethaby's silverware designs
submitted for the Goldsmiths' Hall
Competition are strongly influenced by
Anglo-Flemish work of the sixteenth
century. In the later designs it is the
influence of contemporary work,
particularly that of William Burges which is
most evident. The characteristics of his
subsequent work are best summed up in
Lethaby's own description of eighteenth-
century iron work:
'The method followed is to keep the general
form quite simple and the areas flat, while
the decoration, just an embroidery of the
surface, is one substance and in the
slightest possible relief.'

108
Metalwork
Goldsmiths' Hall Competition, 1882
a. Design for a salad bowl
Pencil and pen (65 × 52)
b. Design for a silver fruit dish
Ink and pencil (65 × 52)
Signed W.R.Lethaby
Private Coll.
The salad bowl design was awarded £10 in
the annual competition organised by
Goldsmiths' Hall. The pseudonym used by
Lethaby in 1882 was 'Vive la Renaissance'.

109
Designs for Metalwork
Goldsmiths' Hall 1883
Dish and ewer in silver
Watercolour and pen (68 × 52)
Signed W.R.Lethaby
Private Coll.
In 1883 Lethaby won £35 for his ewer and
dish in silver and chose the pseudonym of
'Pegasus'.

110
Designs for Metalwork
Goldsmiths' Hall 1884
a. Design for a toilet set in silver
Pen and ink (50 × 73)
b. Design for a toilet glass
Pen and ink (65 × 49)
Signed W.R.Lethaby
Private Coll.
'Argentier' was the pseudonym used by
Lethaby for the 1884 exhibition at
Goldsmiths' Hall.

111
Lead Garden Vase
Designed and executed by W.R.Lethaby
made by Wenham and Waters
Exhibited Arts and Crafts Exhibition
Society 1889 No. 859
Now lost. Original photograph

112
Lead Flower Tub
Designed and executed by W.R.Lethaby
made by Wenham and Waters
Exhibited Arts and Crafts Exhibition
Society 1889 No. 841
Now lost. Original photograph
These are the only known executed designs
for leadwork by Lethaby; he was also
responsible for the modelling.

113
Wedding Ring
Gold. Bezel in form of a church façade, set
with an amethyst, an emerald, and a
sapphire, with a sapphire flanked by rubies
below. Designed by W.R.Lethaby. Made
by H.Wilson. The hoop struck with
Wilson's monogram.
1901
V&A Dept. of Metalwork

109

112

115

114
Haddon Hall
Designs for ironwork and leadwork by
W.R.Lethaby
a. Early ironwork
Pen and ink (38 × 54)
Signed W.R.Lethaby, August 1878
b. Firedogs
Pen and ink (42 × 30)
January 1878. Signed with his monogram.
Private Coll.

Firegrates
Lethaby had a particular feeling for cast
iron and tried to make this humble material
popular. By the end of 1889 he was
designing for three iron masters: Thomas
Elsley, Portland Metal Works, Great
Portland Street; H.Longdon and Co.,
Oxford Street and Yates and Heywood,
Rotherham, as well as the Coalbrookdale
Iron Co. Lethaby's own comments about
the work of the past exactly describes the
quality and elegance of his own. 'The firegrates, both with hobs and close fronts,
that came into use about the middle of the
last century are decorated all over the field
with tiny flutings, beads and leaf
mouldings, sometimes even with little
figure medallions and carry delicacy to its
limit. The better examples are entirely
successful, both in form and in the
ornamentation, which adapted to this new
purpose, does no more than gracefully
acknowledge its debt to the past.'

115
Chimney Piece
Designed by W.R.Lethaby, executed by
Farmer and Brindley
1889
Exhibited Arts and Crafts Exhibition
Society 1889 No. 298
a. Drawing
Pen and ink (30 × 23)
Private Coll.
b. Photograph (GR)

116
Fireplace
Designed by W.R.Lethaby
Medallions modelled by Emmaline Halse,
representing 'Indoor and Outdoor Life'.
Executed by Coalbrookdale Iron Co.

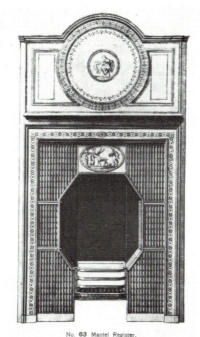

No. **63** Mantel Register.

Loose Bars : Brick at Back : Ashpan Front.

Width over Jambs	...	...	...	...	36-in.
Total Height	...	...	...	...	65½-in.
Height to Shelf	...	...	...	...	44½-in.
Overmantel	...	...	...	...	21-in. high.
Fire	...	...	...	...	12-in.
Shelf	...	...	...	...	34 × 5-in.
Price, Primed	...	...	...	...	115/9 each.

116
Cast iron
1890
Exhibited at the Arts and Crafts Exhibition
Society 1890 No. 461
Photograph from Coalbrookdale Iron Co.
Cat. 1902, Coalbrookdale Museum

117
Designs for metal fireplaces
Four pen and ink drawings on tracing
paper, with notes in Lethaby's hand.
Each (26 × 16)
Private Coll.

118
Two fireplaces in the Central School
Designed by W.R.Lethaby c.1908.
Blue and white tiles possibly by Morris and
Company.
Colour photographs (JM)

Ecclesiastical Design

119
Cartoons for stained glass
St John the Baptist's Church,
Symondsbury, Dorset
1885
a. Photograph of Symondsbury Parish
Church (JM)
b. Photographs of stained glass
c. Saint
Pencil and crayon (189 × 55)
d. Saint
Pencil and crayon (189 × 55)
e. Saint
Pencil and crayon (160 × 33)
f. Saint
Pencil and crayon (160 × 33)
g. Cartoon of entire window
Pencil and crayon
h. Cartoon of upper part of window
Pencil and crayon
V&A Dept. of Prints and Drawings
The iconographical scheme for this very
complex window is taken from the chapter
on the Four Evangelists in Mrs Jameson's
Sacred and Legendary Art.

120
Font
Polished granite
c.1887
All Saints', Leek, Staffs.
Designed by W.R. Lethaby, probably
made by Farmer and Brindley
Photograph (NBR)
Inspired by Byzantine art, the font is
decorated at the base with the symbols of
the Four Evangelists.

121
Font Cover
Church of St John the Baptist, Low
Bentham, Lancaster
Designed by W.R.Lethaby
1889
a. Black & white photograph of church
interior
b. Walnut, surmounted by a globe
framework with gilding (208 × 86)
Church of Saint John the Baptist, Low
Bentham, Lancaster
c. Design for pomegranate
Pencil with colour (20 × 33)
Private Coll.

Low Bentham church was restored by Norman Shaw in 1878; since Lethaby was still in Shaw's office in 1890 it is probable that he received the commission for the new font and cover from his principal. The font bowl is of alabaster, the canopy of walnut surmounted by a globe framework with gilding. The six brackets of scrollwork are carved with interlaced roses and honeysuckle alternately. At this stage of his career, Lethaby's work was still heavily influenced by sources such as the *Hypnerotomachia Poliphili*, see entries 74–77.

There is no catalogue entry 122

123
Altar Cloth
Designed by W.R.Lethaby and executed by students of the Royal College of Art
1911
Photograph (JM)
The altar cloth was designed by Lethaby for the coronation of King George V and Queen Mary in 1911. It is based on a pair

of medieval frontals of white satin damask belonging to the Church of St James, Chipping Campden, Gloucestershire. The frontal is embroidered with a representation of the crucifixion. The major portion of the embroidery has been executed in pure gold and silver thread.

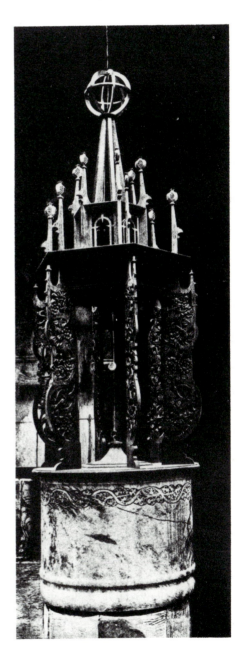

Left: Cartoons for stained glass in St John the Baptist's Church, Symondsbury, Dorset. Above: Font for All Saints' Church, Leek, Staffs.

Below and right: Font cover in the church of St John the Baptist, Low Bentham, Lancaster

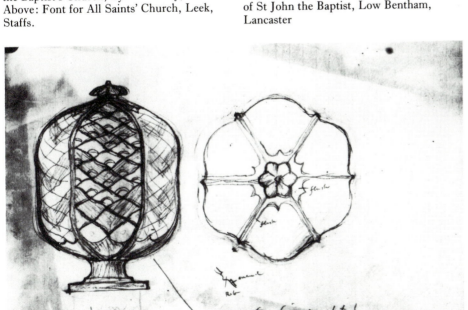

124

Design for chancel screen and stalls
Church of Saint Paul, Four Elms, Kent
1915
Design for chancel screen and stalls
Elevation and sections of mullions, coving
etc. of new screen
Insc.: As above and with notes concerning
construction etc. including '. . . Wood will
be provided/but sent to London for carving
to/a carver I will recommend'
Signed and dated: W.R.Lethaby/111
Inverness Terrace/W/July 6 1915
Pencil and pen (555 × 670)
British Architectural Library, RIBA,
London
Photograph (JM)
The reredos designed by Lethaby and
executed by Stirling Lee and Henry
Pegram is in white marble relief and depicts
the Adoration of the Magi.

Furniture and Interior design

The earliest furniture Lethaby designed
drew on English Renaissance work of the
sixteenth and seventeenth centuries for
inspiration. In 1890 his work for the newly
founded furniture-making co-operative
Kenton and Co. became far more radical.
It was made in solid oak with a variety of
very simple inlays. Lethaby left this
account of Kenton and Co.:
'The group consisted of Macartney and
Blomfield; Gimson and S.Barnsley . . .
Colonel Mallet, a friend of Macartney's
who had "bad taste and knew people" and
finally myself. We each, I believe, put £100
into the business. Taking a workshop in
some court north of Theobald's Road . . .
we engaged an excellent foreman and wrote
"Kenton and Company" on the door. . . .
We enjoyed ourselves greatly for about two
years making many pieces of furniture,
selling some at little over cost price –
nothing being included for design or for the
time expended by the proprietor – and
finally we divided up the remainder at the
end by drawing lots for the first choice.'
Most of the furniture and the designs for
interiors shown here were first seen at the
Arts and Crafts Exhibitions which, since
the Society's foundation in 1888, had been
a focus for Socialist craftsmen and
advanced opinion. The lectures that were

delivered at the annual exhibitions were
subsequently published and formed part of
the growing movement for improved design
and town planning.

125

Stanmore Hall, Stanmore, Middlesex
Design and working drawings for interior
decoration and furnishing by Morris & Co.,
c.1890
a. Perspective of fireplace wall
Insc.: Stanmore Hall: sketch of dining
room and the property of Morris & Co. 449
Oxford Street
Pencil and crayon (500 × 330)
b. Plan, elevation, perspective and detail of
carving table
Insc.: As above and labelled
Pencil and brown crayon (435 × 515)
British Architectural Library, RIBA,
London
c. Photographs (NBR)
d. Design for a carving table c.1891
Photograph (GR)
Lethaby was employed by Morris &
Company on the partial redecoration of
Stanmore Hall in Middlesex, which had
been brought by the Australian millionaire
William Knox D'Arcy. Morris described
the house as 'a house of a very rich man –
and such a wretched uncomfortable place: a
sham Gothic house of fifty years ago . . .'

125

Lethaby designed the five new chimney
pieces, all the woodwork including the
panelling, cupboards, doors, the dog-leg
staircase to the first floor and some built-in
and free-standing furniture. Though badly
damaged, much of the decorative scheme
survives and it is enormously interesting to
see the work of the two men who, a
generation apart, made the most important
contributions to the Arts and Crafts
movement. Lethaby's work is a cool
precursor of a twentieth-century style.

126

**Design for a sash window in grisaille
glass, at Bromley, Kent**
1890
'Spring', Sketch design for sash window
Pen and ink and wash (66 × 51)
Private Coll.
This window in grisaille glass was
described by *The Architect* of 1890 as 'A
modern window for a modern house. The
ornament was intended to suggest nature
and not the past of art.'

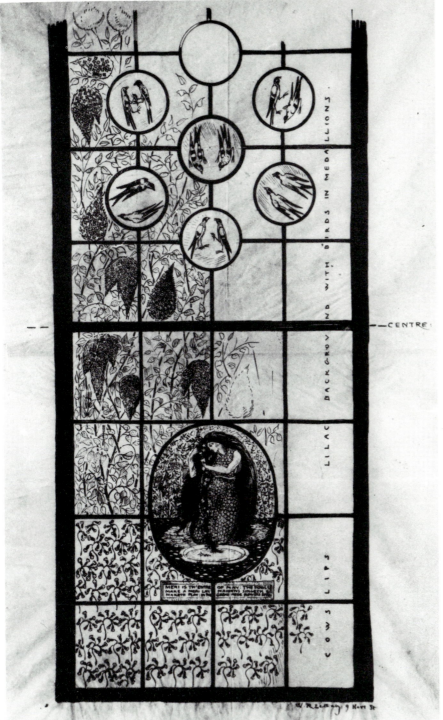

126

127
Kenton and Company
Photograph of William Lethaby (standing)
and Ernest Gimson
1890
Leicester Museum
One of the five active members of Kenton
and Co. Reginald Blomfield, wrote in his
autobiography: 'Lethaby was "as usual our
fount of inspiration" in the foundation of
the company'.

128
Kenton and Company
Photographs
V&A Collection
Photographs (JM)

129
Cupboard
Design for a cupboard by W.R.Lethaby,
executed by Kenton and Co. for Buller's
Wood
1890/91
Pencil (38 × 25)
Private Coll.

130
Bishop's Chair
Designed by W.R.Lethaby, executed by
Kenton and Co.
1891
Oak inlaid with figures of sheep
(169 × 67 × 55)
St John the Baptist's Church, Aldenham,
nr Radlett, Herts.

131
Sewing Box
Designed by W.R.Lethaby, executed by
Kenton and Co.
1890/91
Walnut. Lid inlaid with herringbone design
(29 × 60)
Private Coll.

132
Chest
Designed by W.R.Lethaby, executed by
Kenton and Co.
1890/91
Oak inlaid with sailing ships
(119 × 60 × 50)
Private Coll.

133
**Arts and Crafts Exhibition Society
Minutes before 9 May 1888**
(230 × 180)
Bound by Roger Powell
(letter from him inside front cover, dated
16th May, 1951)
(Lethaby's name included in list of
members)
Roger Powell was an ex-student of the
Central School of Arts and Crafts.

134
**Arts and Crafts Exhibition Society
Minutes of the General Committee
1890–1896**
(235 × 180)
p.64 Lethaby proposed 'That the Society of
Arts be informed that we shall be pleased
for them to select works exhibited at the
"Arts and Crafts" for prizes providing that
this selection be made wholly by themselves
and the works so selected be in no way
distinguished from other work in our
catalogue on exhibition'.
p.184 List of members present at the
committee held at 49 Frognal, on Monday
May 18th, 1896 at 8.00 pm
Walter Crane (in the chair), Benson,
Blomfield, Cobden-Sanderson (Hon. Sec.),
Image, Goscombe-John, Lethaby, Ricardo,
Sumner, Voysey and Walker

135
**Arts and Crafts Exhibition Society
Minutes of the General Committee 18th
July 1917–3rd May, 1923**
(260 × 205)
Victoria & Albert Museum
Minutes of Friday 3rd March, 1922
Lethaby (Vice-President) in the chair
Minutes signed by him (13th March, 1922)

136
Design for interior
By W.R.Lethaby
Unexecuted
Design for room in black and pearl
Exhibited Arts and Crafts Exhibition
Society, 1st exhibition, 1888, No. 443
Watercolour and pencil (33 × 55)
Private Coll.
This design seems to show the influence of
Lethaby's visit to the painter Alma
Tadema's house in 1884 with other
members of the St George's Art Society.

137
**Design for decoration of a room in
panelling and paint**
By W.R.Lethaby
Unexecuted
1888
Watercolour (34 × 65)
Exhibited Arts and Crafts Exhibition
Society, 1st exhibition, 1888
Private Coll.

138
Arts and Crafts Exhibition Society
Photograph of 1890 Arts and Crafts
Exhibition showing furniture by
F.M.Brown, R.Bloomfield, E.Gimson and
W.R.Lethaby
V&A Dept. of Furniture

139
**Arts and Crafts Exhibition Society
Catalogue of the fifth exhibition, 1896**
Photographs (JM)

140
**Photographs of work by W.R.Lethaby
exhibited in the Arts and Crafts
Exhibition 1896 (fifth exhibition)**
Photographs reproduced in *The Studio*
a. Table with marble top, designed by
W.R.Lethaby executed by Farmer and

132

136

Brindley (ACES no. 181)
b. Chimney-piece in marble and onyx
designed by W.R.Lethaby executed by
Farmer and Brindley (ACES no. 149)
c. Firegrate executed by J.Gardner for the
Portland Metal Works (Thomas Elsley)
(ACES no. 150)
d. Firedogs, wrought iron and enamel,
executed by J.Longdon & Co., assisted by
J.Lucas, J.Dyson and P.Atherton (ACES
no. 151)
e. Candlesticks, cast iron and enamel,
executed by J.Longdon & Co. (ACES no.
152)

141
Arts and Crafts Exhibition Society
Invitation card to private view of the eighth
exhibition of the Arts and Crafts Exhibition
Society.
Saturday, January 13th 1906.
Designed by Walter Crane
Private Coll.

137

142
Sideboard
Designed by W.R.Lethaby, executed by
A.Mason
1906
Oak with inlay
Exhibited Arts and Crafts Exhibition
Society, 8th exhibition, No. 291
a. Black and white photograph
b. Drawing for inlay on drawer of sideboard
Pen and ink, pencil (44 × 54)
Private Coll.

143
**Designs for a Memorial Seat to John
Carruthers**
By W.R.Lethaby
1914
a. Design for an oak seat, front and side
view Pen, pencil and watercolour wash
(19 × 45)
b. Design for inscription carved on seat
Pen and ink (30 × 30)
Private Coll.

John Carruthers was a close friend of
William Morris and accompanied Morris on
a sea trip to Norway in the year of Morris's
death 1896.

Design in Industries Association
Increasingly Lethaby was disturbed at the
dirt and disorder of modern cities and the
low level of industrial design. Consequently
he threw his considerable weight behind
such organisations as the British Institute
of Industrial Art and the Design in
Industry Association which he helped
found.
The Design in Industries Association is an
association of manufacturers, designers,
distributors and economists which aims to
improve industrial design and educate the
public. Lethaby was closely involved in its
foundation in 1915.

144
Lethaby, W.R.
Art and Workmanship
First printed in Number 1 of *The Imprint*,
January 1913. Reprinted in this form by
the DIA with the Author's permission,
March 1915
(18 × 10)
Central School Coll.

145
**A proposal for the foundation of a
Design and Industries Association by
W.R.Lethaby.**
Published by the Design for Industry
Association.
c.1914
Unsigned (150 × 180)
British Architectural Library, RIBA,
London

94

142a

142b

Stage Design

146

**Ulysses, a play by Stephen Phillips
stage set designs by W.R.Lethaby**

1902

a. Photograph, University of Bristol,
Theatre Coll.

b. Descriptive Pamphlet
Theatre Collection

c. Model of set by Theatre Design
Department, Central School

d. Museum study of Assyrian Lions from
the British Museum

(50 × 33)

Private Coll.

This play was produced by Beerbohm Tree
at His Majesty's Theatre, London and was
Lethaby's only stage design.

'The sketches for the production were done
by W.R.Lethaby and are intended to give
an idea of that peculiar system of primitive
architecture and decoration the traces of
which have lately been uncovered in
Mycenae and other sites in Greece.' The
descriptive pamphlet produced for the
production comments that Lethaby's
designs freely reflect the general spirit of
the remains discovered. Unfortunately a
number of changes had to be made to his
original designs. Conventional stage
trappings were added, his colours modified
and the position of his buildings changed.

There are no catalogue entries 147 or 148

Lethaby and Education

A large part of Lethaby's life was devoted
to reform. At first this was directed at
architecture and education but later it was
turned towards civilisation itself. While in
Shaw's office he was involved in founding
the St George's Society which was the
prime mover in the creation of the Art-
Workers' Guild. Although it included many
painters, it was the first organisation of
professional designers and became most
influential in art education. The Art-Workers'
Guild was instrumental in founding the Arts
and Crafts Exhibition Society over which
Lethaby presided for a number of years.
Among the first to recognise Lethaby's gifts
as a teacher was Norman Shaw who
recommended him for the appointment of
art inspector in the Technical Education

Board of the newly created London County Council. Appointed in 1894 he and his fellow inspector, the sculptor George Frampton, immediately set about expanding the capital's art education and reorganising existing art schools. The Central School of Arts and Crafts was established in 1896 and run on entirely new lines.

Art-Workers' Guild

Numerous Victorian architects and artists, particularly the young and idealistic, objected to the unrepresentative nature and narrow commercialism of the Royal Institute of British Architects and the Royal Academy. Members of the St George's Art Society campaigned for a society that would bring together painters, architects, sculptors and craftsmen in a new organisation that was dedicated to promoting the cause of art in the widest sense. Their efforts resulted in the founding of the Art-Workers' Guild in 1884.

149
Memorial Plaque
Portrait plaque in the RIBA
Inscribed 'Master AWG 1911'
Photograph (British Architectural Library, RIBA, London)

149

150
Massé, H.L.J.
The Art-Workers' Guild 1884–1934
A history of the Art-Workers' Guild.
Printed at the Shakespeare Head Press, St Aldates, Oxford MCMXXXV.
List of Subjects discussed under Master:
W.R.Lethaby in 1911
Photograph (JM)

151
Master's Chair
Designed by W.R.Lethaby probably for Kenton and Company, executed by G.B.Bellamy.
1893
Oak (137 × 80 × 57)
Art-Workers' Guild
One of two Master's chairs owned by the Art-Workers' Guild

152
'An Account of the Special Meeting held March 31, 1916, by the Art-Workers Guild'
Written by Hugh Arnold and published by the Art-Workers' Guild
40pp illustrated booklet printed by George W.Jones at the Sign of the Dolphin
Private Coll.

153
An illuminated address by W.Graily Hewitt
This address was delivered by the Past Master Selwyn Image before the Art-Workers' Guild on Friday 15th January, MCMIX, being the twenty-fifth anniversary of the Guild's Foundation.
Photograph (JM)

154
Earl of Crawford presenting an address to W.R. Lethaby on his 65th birthday
18 January 1922
Photograph: Private Coll.
Guild

Central School Years

'It was not', in the words of George Clausen, 'that Lethaby taught you how to do anything. He just taught you how to think about the thing.'

151

155
Technical Education Board.
19 November 1894
List of Selected Candidates for Inspectorship of Art Schools and Classes.
Testimonials and References on Lethaby by R.Norman Shaw, William Morris, Sir Edward Burne-Jones, Walter Crane, Philip Webb, Haywood Sumner and W.B.Richmond.
Photograph: GLC Record Office
Mr Norman Shaw says '. . . he has the invaluable quality of influencing for good all with whom he comes in contact. To my certain knowledge he has been brought into close intimacy with many dozens of young students, and there is not one that has not been visibly influenced by him, their work has been improved and their aims have been raised.'

156
Frampton, George
a. Portrait of Charles Keene by George Frampton, signed and dated. Presented by the artist.
1896

154

156b

Bronze (86 × 57 × 6)
Trustees of the Tate Gallery
The sculptor George Frampton was
appointed with Lethaby as joint part-time
Art Inspector in 1894.
b. Sir George Frampton
Photograph (NPG)

157
**Document of Appointment to the Board
of Technical Education; later the LCC**
Issued to W.R.Lethaby in November 1894
Photograph: GLC Record Office

158
**First Central School of Arts and Crafts
316 Regent Street**
Photograph (Private Coll.)
In the years 1896–1907 the Central School
was housed in temporary premises
consisting of 316 Regent Street, a private
house in Little Portland Street and a two-
storey building fronting the same street,
having several large rooms at the rear
rented from the Regent Street Polytechnic
opposite.

159
**Technical Education Board, Central
School of Arts and Crafts**
1. Provisional Prospectus
2. First Prospectus 1896
3. Prospectus 1911
Photographs (JM)

160
LCC **New Building, Southampton Row**
The southern end was originally the
London Day Training College for Teachers
Photograph (JM)

161
**Central School of Arts and Crafts,
Southampton Row**
Ground Plan
Photograph

162
**Photograph of the staff of the Royal
College of Art, c.1905**
Private Coll.
Lethaby was appointed first Professor of
Ornament and Design when the Royal

College was reorganised in 1901 and
continued to act as Principal at the Central
School of Arts and Crafts until 1910.

163
**Memorial Addresses to W.R.Lethaby,
Principal of the Central School of Arts
and Crafts, on his retirement**
1. Address to Professor Lethaby from the
Staff of The Central School. June 1910.
Bound in red leather, tooled in gold.
(28 × 23)
2. Address to Professor Lethaby from the
Students of the Central School. June 1910.
Bound in red leather, tooled in gold.
(28 × 23)
Athenaeum Museum, Barnstaple

164
**Letter from The Education Officer, LCC
on the resignation of W.R.Lethaby
from his position of Art Inspector**
Dated 20 December 1915
Private Coll.

158

PRELIMINARY PROSPECTUS.

London County Council.

TECHNICAL EDUCATION BOARD.

CENTRAL SCHOOL OF ARTS AND CRAFTS,

TEMPORARY PREMISES—

MORLEY HALL, REGENT STREET, W.

(Opposite the Regent Street Polytechnic),

Under the direction of Mr. GEORGE FRAMPTON, A.R.A., and Mr. W. R. LETHABY.

Provisional Prospectus.

The Central School of Arts and Crafts will begin its session on the 21st of October. It provides for apprentices, pupils and workmen engaged in, or connected with, artistic handicrafts the best instruction in art and design *as applied to their particular industries.* No attempt is made to meet the requirements of the amateur, or to do the work of the teacher of figure and landscape drawing and painting; nor is the instruction given directed in any way towards the preparation of pupils for examination. The special business of the school is the industrial application of decorative design, and students are expected to concentrate their studies on the several branches of the industries in which they are engaged.

---

* These arrangements are provisional only, and are subject to such modification as the Technical Education Board may deem advisable.

[T.E. 1608.

163(1)

TO PROFESSOR LETHABY:
on his retiring from the post of Principal of the Central School of Arts & Crafts, from the Masters & Officials at present & in past years engaged there.

Dear Sir:
In giving this formal expression to our regret at your withdrawal from the Superintendence of the School, we wish to assure you of our appreciation of the work you have originated and organized: this work has been, in our opinion, a benefit to the community in general as well as to the Students & ourselves; and we venture to hope that we may still look to you for help in our endeavour to carry on the traditions which you have inaugurated.
Besides regretting your withdrawal from the School on general grounds, each one of us has a private, personal grief at losing a Master so gracious, helpful, & illuminative. We trust that in the years to come the conduct of the School will still be such that you may reflect on your creation with satisfaction.

We are, Dear Sir, Yours faithfully

The Staff of the Central School of Arts & Crafts:

162

TO PROFESSOR W. R. LETHABY, ON HIS RESIGNATION OF THE POST OF PRINCIPAL, OF THE LONDON COUNTY COUNCIL CENTRAL SCHOOL. OF ARTS AND CRAFTS.

It is with much regret that we, the Students of the Central School of Arts and Crafts, hear of your intended resignation, from the Post of Principal. We should like to thank you for the help you have given to our work, as well as to express our warm admiration for what you have done in spreading ideals of good design united with craftmanship. by means of the technical classes of London. We feel that although deprived of your direct influence in the future. the traditions you have established will remain as a lasting stimulus to the School.

Eveleen Buckton
Phyllis Frood.
Harold K Wolfenden
Dr I Humphreys
Leonard Jay
John. E. Tarbeaux
Mabel Coplin.
William Weinhart.
H. J. Whitmee.
Cecilia Adams.
M. Collings
Mabel Levy
E. Horwitz
R. Bray.
A. Berryman

W Holloway
J McVittie
W H Green
A H Hancock
Cecil V. Thomas
C. W. Turley
J Minihane
John H. W. Brandt.
W^m A Jutting
W. Willingale
J A Webb
Charles Whitfield
Philip G. Esmond.
F Wildash
Frank L Emanuel

Helen R. Wilson
I. J. Curman
Florence W. Cash.
Frank White
Edith Ludgate
Alfred H. Wilkinson.
Gabriel Bunney
Ellewell. Hill.
Charles J. Bathurst
Katherine A M. Pearce
Ethel R. Curwen.
Sydney R. Turner
Edward N Reader
J. J. Biskop.
Alfred C Welch.

163(2)

Technical Education Board Collection of Schools Examples

In the second half of the nineteenth century students of fine art and design made frequent use of examples, both museum specimens and reproductions, for the purpose of study and inspiration. Many London Museums such as the South Kensington Museum, the Westminster Museum and the British Museum, authorised reproduction in the form of plaster casts, engravings and photographs for use in schools of art. Students could also visit collections of casts and facsimiles such as the Historic Art Courts of the Crystal Palace where they could see 'the finest collection in the world of examples showing the development of art, as applied in architecture and decoration, and as affected by the climate, materials and history of each country'.

The newly formed Technical Education Board of the LCC was particularly concerned with providing a wide range of examples to design students. In February and March 1894 the Special Sub-Committee on Art and Technology of the Board empowered Professor J.H.Middleton, the Director of the South Kensington Museum, to purchase art examples to the sum of £500 for the Board during the course of his five-week tour of the Continent. A lengthy letter was sent from the Secretary stipulating the type of examples the Board wished to circulate to schools of art specialising in design. These included museum specimens and reproductions, particularly facsimiles, photographs and plaster casts. Special concern was voiced regarding the poor quality of plaster casts currently used by students. The Board felt that an improved collection would enliven classes of modelling and decorative design. Lethaby and Frampton, in their rôle as art inspectors to the Board, put forward a suggestion that several rooms of the Board's Technical School at Bolt Court be assigned to the examples and also recommended that the collection be indexed and fully labelled 'with every particular of material, methods, position, etc.' The inspectors also requested that a casting shed be equipped to make up examples drawn from museums. From this date, Lethaby undertook the purchase of

examples, reporting sporadically to the Board on his acquisitions. The collection was moved to the Central School of Arts and Crafts, Regent Street, in 1896 and was to follow the School to its new premises in Holborn. Twenty years after the formation of the Board's collection, F.V.Burridge, the second Principal of the Central School, organised an exhibition of the collection in order to rekindle interest in this fascinating circulating library.

165
Benedict
Reguli sanctissimi patris mostri Benedicti
Manuscript on vellum
Bound in vellum with illuminated initials
(27 × 22)
LCC School Examples Collection
Central School Coll.

166
Poggio, Jacopo
Historica Fiorentina da Latino in nostra lingua tradocta da Iacopo suo Figliovolo
Venice, Rossi, 1476
First two pages in manuscript with coloured and gilt initial (32 × 22)
LCC Schools Examples Collection
Central School Coll.

167
Herbarius in Latin
Mainz, Schoeffer, 1484
Illustrated with handcoloured woodcuts
Rebound at the Central School of Arts and Crafts by F.Garrett and P.R.Sykes c.1910
Calf on oak boards inlaid with rosewood
(25 × 18)
LCC Schools Examples Collection. 3.9.1896
Central School Coll.

168
Roderic Sancti
Clipeus Monarchae Ecclesio
15th-century manuscript
Written by an Italian scribe on vellum and paper, with illuminated initial and arabesque border, half calf (26 × 23)
LCC Schools Examples Collection
Central School Coll.

167

172

169
Sallustius, Crispus
C. Crispi Sallusti opera
Paris, John du Pré, 1521
(17 × 10)
LCC Schools Examples Collection 3.9.1896
Central School Coll.

170
Petrarch
Poems
Venice, Aldus, 1546
Full morocco binding (17 × 10)
LCC Schools Examples Collection
25.10.1897
Central School Coll.

171
Roberius, Hieronymus
Quod animalia bruta ratione ulantur melius
Homine
Paris, Cramoisy, 1648
Bound in old red morocco with gold tooling
LCC Schools Examples Collection
Central School Coll.

172
Curtis, William
Flora Londinensis, or plates and
descriptions of such plants as grow wild in
the environs of London.
Vol. I.
London, Curtis, 1777
Many handcoloured plates (45 × 28)
LCC Schools Examples Collection
Central School Coll.

173
Illuminated manuscripts
Details: 2 small double frames
1. (34 × 21)
2. (39 × 20)
LCC Schools Examples
Central School Coll.

174
Viollet-le-Duc
Rational Building. Being a translation of
the article 'Construction' in the
*Dictionnaire Raisonné de l'Architecture
Française*, by George Martin Huss.
Macmillan & Co., London. 1895
(21 × 17)
LCC Schools Examples Collection
24.11.1896
Central School Coll.

**Collection of the Central School of Arts
and Crafts**
In July 1896 the Technical Education
Board appropriated £200 to the Art
Inspectors to purchase art examples for the
proposed Central School of Arts and
Crafts. Thereafter as Principal, Lethaby
was to enlarge the School's own collection
considerably through purchases and
bequests.

175
Illuminations
Selection of illuminated initials: French,
Italian and Dutch, of the fourteenth and
fifteenth centuries.
Central School Coll.

176
The Nuremberg Chronicle
Latin edition 1493
pages 253 and 267
(43 × 30)
Central School Coll.

177
Dürer, Albrecht
The Last Supper. From the Great Passions
series.
1511 ed. pub. Dürer.
Woodcut (40 × 28)
Central School Coll.

178
Morris, William
Well at the World's End quarto sheet
Kelmscott Press
(57 × 41)
Central School Coll.

179
William de Morgan
Tiles
a. (20 × 33)
b. (20 × 20)
Tin-glazed earthenware tiles
Central School Coll.

180
Rooke, Noel
Details of 15th-century Flemish tapestry at
South Kensington, 1899
Watercolour (27 × 22)
Central School Coll.

177

179

181
Stencils
Japanese
4 examples
(40 × 25)
Central School Coll.

182
Japanese triptych
Early 19th-century painting of three actors,
one man and two women
(38 × 74)
Central School Coll.

183
Woodblocks
Japanese, partially cut. 20th century
a. (15 × 8)
b. (18 × 12)
Central School Coll.

184
Ruskin, John
Leaves
Thought to be engraved for *Modern
Painters*, Vol. IV, plate 43.
Pencil and watercolour
(16 × 29)
Central School Coll.

185
Morris, William
Wallpaper sample
Fruit. 1864
(also known as Pomegranate)
(56 × 66)
Central School Coll.

186
Jacquard weaving
1 fragment
(33 × 21)
Central School Coll.

187
Ecclesiastical embroidery
Dark red silk, embroidered
(58 × 50)
Central School Coll.

188
Hogarth, William
The analysis of beauty
London, J.Reeves, 1753
This edition has folding plates and is bound
in leather.
(26 × 21)
From the Library of the Female School of
Art, 1859
Central School Coll.

189
Rhead, G.W.
Alphabet of Roman Capitals, together with
3 sets of lower-case letters, selected and
enlarged from finest examples and periods.
For Schools 1903
Central School Coll.

190
Page of Italian 15th-century altar book
Rotunda hand, Lombardic versals,
illuminated initial S with scrollwork and
gilding
(15 × 10)
Central School Coll.

Central School Staff and Students

The Central School of Arts and Crafts
introduced to London an entirely new
concept of design education. For the first
time teaching was conducted by practising
architects, artists and craftsmen in specially
equipped workshops. Students learned to
design through the mastery of tools and
materials, and only craftsmen and
apprentices were granted admission. The
first staff members included some of the
most eminent craftworkers of the day.
Although Lethaby was not officially
appointed until 1902 he had been *de facto*
principal since the School opened.
As early as July 1895 Lethaby had
submitted a report to the Technical
Education Board in which he spoke of
'architectural design which shall not be
taught in reference to archaeology but
which may be distinguished by the name of
positive or constructive architecture'.
Although it has been impossible to trace
relevant work for this exhibition, the
architecture and building classes formed
the initial core of classes at the Central
School. Halsey Ricardo was head of the
architecture department, assisted after 1897
by R.B.Molesworth, who taught the
mechanics of building. Until 1905,
E.Roscoe Mullins conducted classes in
modelling and ornament as applied to
architecture and the allied crafts. Other
staff from the early days of the Central
included R.H.Hook (stone working for
architects), Percy R.Kirk, R.Garbe, Percy

N.Ginham and S.B.Caulfield. In 1905
structural mechanics (E.Sprague) and
building construction (F.H.Mansford)
were added to the syllabus. The
department seems to have expanded in
1908 with the arrival of P.J.Waldram
(structural mechanics), Noel Heaton
(chemistry of materials) and F.Lessore
(decorative plasterwork). A review of 1909
in *The Building News* complained of 'an
endeavour on the part of the teachers to
impress students with the cult of simplicity,
carried to the extreme of showing bare
construction without satisfactory and
necessary ornament . . .'.

191
Central School Staff and Students
Department of Architecture
a. Ricardo, Halsey (1854–1928)
Photographs (JM)
1. Graffham, nr. Petworth, Sussex. 1905–7
2. The Eyot House, Sonning-on-Thames.
3. Design for a small country house
4. House at Letchworth Garden City
b. Garbe, Richard
Portrait
Photograph (JM)

Leadwork and metalwork
Francis W.Troup (an architect) assisted by
the registered plumber William Dodds
taught leadwork at the Central School
1896–1900. Lethaby took a special interest
in this subject; his book *Leadwork* was
published in 1893. After her visit to the
Central School in 1897 Esther Wood
recounted: 'It is a matter for regret that no
plumbers have yet joined the decorative
lead-work that is known to be a special
study with the architects; but it is hoped
that in this instance a demand may be
created by the supply, and the plumbers
may be attracted to the subject. It should
be noted, however, that the practical side of
plumbing, in its sanitary and domestic
branches, is taught with equal
thoroughness. With the assistance of Mr
Dodds, the instruction is made to include
the treatment of roofs and everything
usually specified as "external plumbing".
But the purpose of the decorative study is
to give the craftsman a new interest in, and
love of, the material itself; and in the

working of lead – one of the most barren and uninteresting of substances to the ordinary worker – there is certainly scope for development of this kind.'

In 1908 classes in ironwork (A.W.Elwood) and bronze casting (F.Parlanti) were added to the syllabus.

In an obituary for Lethaby, Troup recalled his days in the Central School Lead classes: '. . . seeing some simple cast lead weights of mine in the Arts and Crafts Exhibition, he hoisted me into the classes of the Technical Education Board to work out from old records or any source I could strike, the methods used by the old plumbers in their craft of leadwork and carry on classes on this subject'.

192
Rainhead
Designed by F.W.Troup. Executed by W.Dodd.
Postcard from F.W.Troup
W.R.Lethaby.
Private Coll.

Stained Glass
Christopher Whall, who was one of the staff in the first session of the Central School, shared many of Lethaby's views: 'We are too scholastic. We have learnt too much about styles and periods, and about what was done in Greece or in Florence in this century or the other, instead of studying the principles of art itself, and how to take direct from nature all that we want for decoration and symbolic design.' Other teachers in stained glass appointed by Lethaby were A.J.Drury (1900), J.H.Stanley (1902), G.F.Brodrick (1902) and Karl B.Parsons (1904).

193
'Patterns for lead glazing by C. Whall and his pupils – January, 1900'
2pp introduction and 12pp of designs
Published by the author with Messrs. Lowndes and Drury of 35, Park Walk, SW3
Private Coll.

194
A.J.Drury
Photograph

192

195
Nelson, Benjamin
Penelope weaving.
Stained glass panel (40 × 34)
Private Coll.

196
Karl B.Parsons
Photograph

197
Parsons, Karl
a. Stained glass panel. Copy of window at Chartres twelfth century. 'Descent from the Cross' (23 cm diam.)
Private Coll.
Karl Parsons probably used this panel to demonstrate techniques of medieval glass-making in his classes at the Central School of Art
b. Reproduction of the original window

198
Arnold, Hugh
Sketch design for heraldic window in the Hatton Chapel, All Saints' Church, Long Stanton, Cambs. 1907
Watercolour, ink and pencil (40 × 27)
Private Coll.

Hugh Arnold attended Christopher Whall's stained glass classes at the Central School from February 1898 – June 1903; he wrote one of the classics of stained glass literature, *Stained Glass of the Middle Ages in England and France* (1913) and made windows for churches throughout the UK. He was killed on active service at Gallipoli in 1915.
Private Coll.

199
Esplin, Mabel
Stained glass roundel depicting boy with rabbits, by a former Central School student.
c.1912 (33 cm in diameter)
Private Coll.

Woodwork and Furniture
Classes in woodcarving and gilding were undertaken by F.Stuttig and R.P.Underwood in 1899; Charles Spooner conducted the teaching in design for cabinet makers. Cabinet work and wood-inlay classes were started by P.A.Wells in 1900. In 1901, *The Artist* commented favourably on work by Central students in the carving and gilding of picture frames; traditional methods were being revived as opposed to the prevailing modern techniques of die-moulded ornament. The furniture-making department of the School expanded considerably in 1908 with the addition of polishing and upholstery classes. George Jack joined the staff in the same year.

200
Jack, George
a. Music Cabinet with carved panel
Designed by George Jack, executed by George Jack and Lawrence Turner
c.1909 (the panel 1900)
Light oak (144 × 102 × 42)
William Morris Museum, Walthamstow
Exhibited at the 1910 Arts & Crafts Exhibition
b. Drawing for part of a carved panel for the centre part of the panel in the music cabinet
By George Jack
A ewe and a ram amidst foliage
Pencil (19 × 16)
William Morris Gallery, Walthamstow
c. Photograph
Arts & Crafts Society Exhibition 1910

200

George Jack was Philip Webb's clerk and after Webb's death worked for the LCC Architecture Department and at the Central School of Arts and Crafts.

201
Furniture Designs
Student sketch books n.d.
a. (22 × 13)
b. (22 × 13)
Central School Coll.

Writing and Illumination
Edward Johnston began his classes in writing and illumination at the Central School in 1899 and continued these for the duration of Lethaby's Principalship. Commenting on this, one of Lethaby's most inspired appointments, Sir Sydney Cockerell was to say 'If a young man came to *me* with work like that, I should tell him there was no hope for him!'
Additional classes commenced in 1902

under W. Graily Hewitt. Johnston was to have an extraordinary impact on his students; Eric Gill recalled: 'On that evening I was thus rapt. It was no mere dexterity that thus transported me; it was as though a secret of heaven were being revealed.'
The Central School prospectus for 1907 announced that 'special attention will be devoted to the requirements of documents, addresses, and, above all, the book, as to

Furniture designs from students' sketchbooks

the proportion of margins to text, size of letter, spacing of lines, capitals to paragraphs, beginnings and endings, etc.'

202
Johnston, Edward
6 photographs of a blackboard demonstration
These photographs demonstrate the use of Foundational hand, how to cut quills, page layout, illumination and decoration etc.
Central School Coll.

203
Teaching Sheets
A selection of jelly prints produced by Johnston for his classes.
This material was used as the basis for his book *Writing, Illuminating and Lettering.*

204
Johnston, Edward
Manuscript and Inscription Letters for schools and classes & for the use of craftsmen by Edward Johnston with 5 plates by A.E.R.Gill. Ninth impression, 1950.
Folder of 16 plates
(32 × 36)
Central School Coll.

205
Diploma of Fellowship of the Central School of Arts and Crafts
Written by Edward Johnston and engraved by George Friend. Intended to honour outstanding designer craftsmen and awarded among others to Eric Gill and Alfred Fairbank.
(35 × 22)
Central School Coll.

206
Block letter alphabet
a. Block letter alphabet for London Underground.

Working drawing. Spring 1916
(26 × 22)
b. Numerals. Working drawing
(50 × 75)
Central School Coll.
In the spring of 1916 Johnston designed his block letter alphabet for Frank Pick for London Underground. Pick wanted 'The bold simplicity of the authentic lettering of the finest periods' and yet to belong to the twentieth century. Johnston's letters have been credited with bringing about a revolution in printing. Johnston himself recognised the historic importance of these letters which he had based on classical

Roman capital proportions: 'It is in fact the foundational model of *all modern*, respectable Block letters . . .'
c. Photographs: 2 black and white

207
The Trajan Column, Rome, c.AD 114
Inscription incised in a marble panel 4ft. 6in. by 10ft. above ground level.
Photograph
Under Edward Johnston the Trajan model re-emerged as a standard in letter design. Lethaby had separate casts made from the V&A plaster cast of the Column which provided models of 19 letters in large size so that students could more easily see and draw the forms.

208
Postcard giving instructions to students
6th October 1899
(12 × 9)
Central School Coll.
Sent by Mr Beckett, the School Secretary,
to the members of Johnston's 3rd class.

209
**Letters from Edward Johnston to
Veronica Whall who attended
Johnston's classes at the Central
School.**
Private Coll.

210
Johnston, Edward
Notes on Mrs Mahoney's exercise book
Photographs
Central School Coll.

211
Rooke, Noel
LCC School Certificate for the educational
year 1915–16 (when prizes were suspended
because of the War)
(35 × 29)
Lithographic reproduction in colour,
designed by Noel Rooke
Private Coll.

212
Gill, Eric
Four blueprints of Roman alphabets
(144 × 100)
Photograph
Central School Coll.

213
Gill, Eric
Alphabet and numerals
Plaster cast of marble plaque. The original
cut by Eric Gill.
Signed ERG '09
Central School Coll.
Specimen Roman and Italic lower case
alphabets with numerals.

Metalwork – Gold and Silversmithing
The first appointment to teach
silversmithing at the Central School was
W.Augustus Steward. In its early years, the
silver- and goldsmithing classes were
among the largest in the school. Close links
were maintained with the trade, and

215a

215b

teachers included: Charles Welch,
C.A.Duffy, T.F.Smith, Onslow Whiting,
George Friend, Stephen J.Whittaker,
Albert J.Wilkins, F.Signorelli and
E.T.W.Ware. A Day Technical School for
Boys was proposed for the 1906–07 session.

214
Wilson, Henry
Chafing dish and stand
Designed and made by Henry Wilson,
London 1908/9
Silver with applied gold decoration
(29 cm high)
V&A Handley Read Collection

215
W.Augustus Steward
a. Caskets, designed by W.Augustus
Steward and made by E.Robinson and
C.Russell
b. Silver cups, designed by W.Augustus
Steward and wrought by C.Wiggins
Photographs

216
**Pen sketches from objects by Day
Students (age 14 years) at the Central
School of Arts and Crafts**
Photograph

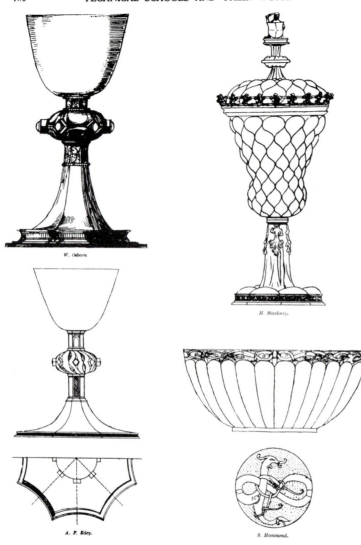

W. Osborn.

H. Stanbury.

A. F. Edey.

S. Hammond.

216

Pen Sketches from Objects by Day Students (age 14 years) at the Central School of Arts and Crafts.

218

217
Alexander Fisher
a. Tryptich in steel and translucent enamel (1897)
b. Electric bracket in steel, silver and bronze with enamel (1900)
Photographs

Painting on China
Alfred Powell taught china painting at the Central School from 1906 to 1908. Miss M. Hindshaw was appointed in 1908 to continue the classes in china painting and design.

218
Powell, Alfred
Painting a ceramic bowl.
Photograph (JM)

Needlework
Lethaby strongly felt the need to revive the art of needlework: 'needlework, which is still practised traditionally in every house, was once a splendid art, an art in which English workers were especially famous'. In the second session of the Central School he employed Maggie Briggs to teach embroidery, Ellen Wright took over the teaching in 1899 directed by May Morris, a visitor to the School.

Enamelling
Alexander Fisher, who taught at the Central School until 1899, was regarded by his contemporaries as having rediscovered the art of enamelling. 'In a class held by Mr McDalpayrat at South Kensington in 1885, Mr Fisher was the only student who took up the subject so seriously as to find in it his ultimate profession; and the absence either of companions or rivals in the field has perhaps favoured his independent experiment and research, stimulating him to re-discover alone – or with the help of a few historical treatises – the secrets of the old Limoges enamellers, and to adapt them to the opportunities of a new industrial craft.' Fisher was succeeded at the Central School in 1899 by R.E.Atkins. After 1900 it was B.Nelson and R.D.Winter who took charge of the classes.

Miss E. Richey started classes in lacemaking in 1905 and dressmaking was added in 1906 by Mrs F. Burgess. As early as 1896 the TEB had stipulated that 'students in textiles will have before them fine old and modern examples, as well as living flowers and plants as aids to their studies'. The Board arranged that the Chief Officer of the parks department should circulate plants to classes, including those in Regent Street. In addition, Central students were granted free admission tickets to the Royal Botanic Society's garden.

219

219
Morris, May
Embroidered frieze, showing small trees, flowers and insects and a small panel of a view from Kelmscott Manor, running verses in Gothic script and a narrow decorative border top and bottom.
Coloured wools on coarse linen (70 × 279)
Signed M.M.
William Morris Gallery, Walthamstow

220
Morris, May
Drawings and annotations on her designs for embroideries
4 designs: Photographs
William Morris Gallery, Walthamstow

221
Brandon-Jones, Anne
Needlework, Alexandra roses, rose-hips, leaves, thorns and buds. Executed in shades of pink and green with a geometric border of green and pink.
(26 × 25)
Private Coll.
Anne Brandon-Jones was a student at the Central School c.1913

222
Willis, Ethel M.
Copy of fragment of brocade, woven in green, pale red and white silk and silver gilt thread on purplish blue satin ground.
North Italian (Lucca) 14th century
Signed E.Willis 03
Watercolour on paper (562 × 457)
V&A, Dept. of Prints & Drawings

Printmaking
Frank Morley Fletcher was employed in 1897 to teach classes in woodcuts in colour. Around the turn of the century, his classes were enormously popular. While acknowledging a debt to Japanese techniques, Fletcher insisted that students discover their own approach to the medium. The classes were temporarily suspended in 1904, then resumed in 1905 by Sidney Lee. George S.Smithard started the first classes in lithography in 1900 (these were restricted to those already working in the trade) and was succeeded in 1902 by F.E.Jackson. L.Taylor, RE, took charge of etching and mezzotint in 1908.

223
Fletcher, Frank Morley
Girl Reading
1900
Colour woodcut (190 × 157)
V&A, Dept. of Prints & Drawings

224
Jackson, F.E.
Flower arrangements
Lithographs printed in colour.
Two lithographs, mounted together, each (21 × 27)
Signed but undated
British Museum, Dept. of Prints & Drawings

225
Rooke, Noel
The Bridge
Woodcut (277 × 205)
Signed, undated
Rooke attended classes at the Central School for five years working under Edward Johnston. Fellow students in the class were Eric Gill, Cobden-Sanderson and Graily Hewitt. During this time Rooke did much research into the revival of wood engraving. He started his wood engraving class at the Central School in 1905; he also taught composition, book illustration, poster and advertisement design.
On the revival of wood-engraving, Noel Rooke was to say: 'Three persons should be mentioned who gave encouragement when it was most needed: Mr Edward Johnston, the scribe; but for him, not so many people would have become engravers as is the case; Professor Lethaby, and Mr Geoffrey Whitworth, who tried very hard to persuade his firm to break new ground.'
British Museum, Prints & Drawings Coll.

226
Taylor, Luke
In the meadows
Etching (175 × 212)
Signed in pencil
British Museum, Prints & Drawings Coll.

227
Lee, Sydney
The Bridge
1908. Signed Sydney Lee
Colour print from woodblocks (153 × 178)
V&A Dept. of Prints & Drawings

228
Lanchester, Edith M.
King Wenceslas
c.1908
Colour woodcut (155 × 79)
V&A Dept. of Prints & Drawings
Edith Lanchester was a student at the
Central School in 1901

Women at the Central School of Arts and Crafts
The Women's Industrial Council reported
in 1905 that the standard of technical
education for girls remained below the level
for boys:
'though it is true that women are invading
men's employment in many directions, they
are rarely to be found working at precisely
the same branches of one trade . . .
Moreover, it is unsafe to assume that
because women are employed in skilled
trades, they perform the skilled branches.
More often the skilled parts are done by
men, and the unskilled by women.'

The education at the Central School,
however revolutionary in certain respects,
was no exception; indeed, the close links
(advocated by Lethaby) between the trades
and classes at the Central often resulted in
the exclusion of women students. Many of
the trades did not admit women (e.g.
bookbinding, gold and silversmithing,
furniture) and thus they were unable to
attend evening classes at the Central in
these subjects. On one occasion, a
prospective female bookbinding student
was informed by the School that both the
bookbinders' and silversmiths' trades had
threatened to withdraw all their men from
the classes if women were admitted. Classes
in drawing and modelling from the life also
created difficulties: in the first five years of
the School's existence, female students
presented a steady stream of petitions
complaining of inadequate teaching.
Women staff were mainly to be found in
embroidery and needlework, miniature and
china painting and dressmaking and
costume. In the academic year 1908–1909
the Royal Female School of Art (formerly
in Queen Square) was amalgamated with
the Central School, but these staff also
tended to specialise in crafts considered
more suitable for ladies. Special afternoon
classes were arranged at the Central for

these apparently less serious subjects.
Despite these obstacles, women students at
the Central seem to have attracted public
notice: a visitor in 1897 commented on the
preponderance of women students in the
stained glass classes, and women from
various departments frequently exhibited
their works outside the School.

229
**Women at the Central School of Arts
and Crafts**
1. Photograph of Life Modelling Class.
2. Photograph of Sculpture by Miss Amy
Wilkins.

School of Book Production
In 1916 *The Studio* was able to report of
the Central School: 'A book can be
produced in its studios and workrooms
complete in every respect – printing,
illustrations, and binding . . .'. The first
classes in book production were those in
bookbinding established in 1897 by
Douglas B.Cockerell, acting on the advice
of Cobden Sanderson. Cockerell was
assisted in his teaching by George Adams.
In 1900 classes in the cleaning and
repairing of books and manuscripts were
added. Other teachers were to join the
staff: J.A.Adams, A.De Sauty, and

229(1)

229(

P.McLeish. A Day Technical School of Book Production was established in 1909. J.H.Mason, who had started his classes in printing and typography in 1905, paid tribute to Lethaby's vision:
'The achievement of Professor Lethaby consisted in recognising that the private press movement was doomed to ultimate failure unless those sound principles of craftsmanship which it had rediscovered could be taught again and applied to an industry which was rapidly being transformed by the age of the machine ... his most original and important contribution lay in the recognition of the Printing School as the one institution unaffected by commercialism, and so able to supplement the inadequate training given to the apprentices of the time with a grounding in those values which alone can define and revivify the true course of good printing.'

230
Cockerell, Douglas
Book Paper Examples
Probably by Douglas Cockerell
Selection of 6 (37 × 30)
Central School Coll.

231
Cesnola, A.P.Di
Salaminia: the history, treasure and antiquities of Salamis in the island of Cyprus. Published and printed by Whiting & Co. London 1884
Bound by George Sutcliffe in the LCC Central School of Arts and Crafts c.1912. Dark green leather tooled in gold and red with tooled gold spine.
(26 × 18)
Central School Coll.

232
Ashbee, C.R.
Conradin: a philosophical ballad
Printed and published by the Essex House Press. 1908.
Limited edition of 250 copies of which this copy is no. 143
Bound and decorated by A.J.Vaughan of the Day Technical School of Book Production, 1912. Dark red leather, tooled in gold (25 × 19)
Central School Coll.

233
Bacon, Francis
Of Adversity
Pages 3–10 dated 1906. Unbound.
These are the first printed pages produced by Central School students under J.H.Mason
Central School Coll.

234
Bacon, Francis
Of Death
Printed at the LCC Central School of Arts and Crafts
Compositor: W.Ellis. Finished Feb. 1909
(23 × 17)
Central School Coll.

235
Bacon, Francis
Of Gardens
Printed at the LCC Central School of Arts and Crafts.
Compositor: C.H.Fein. Decorated by Phyllis Frood.
Process blocks by the LCC School of Photo-Engraving at Bolt Court E.C. Finished May 1909.
(23 × 17)
Central School Coll.

236
Central School of Arts and Crafts School of Book Production and Printing
Specimens of title pages
Photographs: 3 (JM)

237
An Ordinal of Bookbinding and Finishing
Printed at the LCC Central School of Arts and Crafts Day Technical School of Book Production by D.S.Hayward. Teacher J.H.Mason. 1911
(24 × 19)
Central School Coll.

238
Walker, Emery
A Brief History of Printing
Printed at the LCC Central School of Arts and Crafts by A.V.Denham. Instructor, J.H.Mason. March 1911.
(23 × 17)
Central School Coll.

239
Catalogue of a book exhibition at the Central School of Arts and Crafts. With a short account of the History of the LCC classes in book production: May 13 MCMXII
Printed at Central School of Arts and Crafts; Map by H.K.Wolfenden; block by the Bolt Court School. Monogram designed and cut on wood by W.F.Northend. Printed at the School by the Day Technical School of Book Production. 1912
(23 × 15)
Central School Coll.

240
Publi Vergili Maronis
Georgicon Libri Quattuor
Printed and bound at the LCC Central School of Arts and Crafts. 1910. Red leather binding with CSAC monogram.
(22 × 17)
Central School Coll.

241
Pope, Alexander
The rape of the lock: an Heroi-Comical Poem
Printed at the LCC Central School of Arts and Crafts.
Set in Type, Sheet a, by C.H.Fein; sheets b to end, by boys of the Day Technical School of Book Production who entered in 1911. Teacher J.H.Mason 1912.
Bound by S.H.Cole and decorated by A.L.Hackman under the instruction of Peter McLeish. Brown leather binding, tooled in gold.
(23 × 17)
Central School Coll.

242
Hugo, Victor
Sara at the bath
Printed at the LCC Central School of Arts and Crafts by F.W.Woodroof, P.Bayliss and W.Turner, of the Day Technical School of Book Production. Teacher, J.H.Mason. Initial letters drawn by Muriel Browne, in the Book Illustration Class; engraved on wood by Leonard Searle and A.Pruden of the Day Technical School, Teacher Noel Rooke. 1912.
a. Bound in pale grey boards with cloth spine (25 × 18)

240

b. Bound by B.J.Cronk, decorated by
G.M.Wickman under the instruction of
P.McLeish. Brown leather tooled in gold
(25 × 19)
Central School Coll.

243
Three Psalms, LVI: CXXI: CXII
Printed at the LCC Central School of Arts
and Crafts by the Day Technical School of
Book Production.
Teacher, J.H.Mason. Blocks drawn and cut
on the wood by Vivien Gribble under Noel
Rooke, September 1912.
Bound by Middleton and decorated by
Matthews. Undyed cow hide, tooled. n.d.
(38 × 25)
Central School Coll.

244
Spenser, Edmund
Four Hymns on earthly and heavenly love
and beauty
Printed at the LCC Central School of Arts
and Crafts: sheet a by W.F.Northend;
sheets b, c, d, e, f, g by the Day Technical
School of Book Production, Initial L drawn
and cut by W.F.Northend. Initials A and
W, by A.G.Pruden under Noel Rooke.
Printing teacher, J.H.Mason. 1913
Bound and decorated by R.J.Gardiner
under the instruction of P.McLeish. Brown
leather binding, tooled in gold with leather
end papers in dark blue and brown tooled
in gold. n.d.
(28 × 21)
Central School Coll.

245
**The Autobiography (1706–57) of
Benjamin Franklin**
Printed at the Central School of Arts and
Crafts. Sheets a, b, c by W.Hyland and
S.Collins (evening students) in 1910–11;
sheets d to end by the boys of the Day
Technical School of Book Production.
Teacher, J.H.Mason. Finished 1913.
Frontispiece engraved on wood in the
Illustration Class by Phyllis Seale from a
painting by F.Baricolo after a portrait by
J.S.Duplessis (1783)
a. Bound by Benkoski and decorated by
Mattheas under the instruction of Peter
McLeish.
Dark green leather binding tooled in gold.
Decorative endpapers.
(28 × 20)
b. Bound under the instruction of
P.McLeish. 1916 Dark green leather tooled
in gold.
(28 × 20)
c. Bound and decorated by R.J.Gardiner
under the instruction of P.McLeish. Brown
leather binding, tooled. Leather end papers.
(28 × 20)
Central School Coll.

246
Wordsworth, William
Laodamia. 1814
Printed at the LCC Central School of Arts
and Crafts. Set in type by John Whelan.
Teacher, J.H.Mason. 1913
Bound in deep plum coloured leather,
tooled in gold. n.d.
(25 × 18)
Central School Coll.

247
The Imprint
Published at the Central School from
January to September 1913 (9 issues in all)
T.J.Cobden-Sanderson, F.E.Jackson,
Edward Johnston and J.H.Mason were
responsible for this new printing journal of
wider outlook than those already existing.
The newly designed type was cut by the
Lanston Monotype Company and
christened 'Imprint Old Face'. The
editorial of the first issue stated 'We . . .
congratulate the Monotype Company on
having produced the finest face that has
been put upon the market in modern times'.
Central School Coll.

The Imprint

February 17th, 1913

MY BOOKS FOR CHILDREN: By WALTER CRANE
PRINTING OF CHILDREN'S BOOKS: By J. H. MASON
THE ILLUSTRATION OF CHILDREN'S BOOKS: By
Alice Meynell; H. Belloc; Clarence Rook; Arthur Waugh;
Barry Pain; J. P. Collins; Edward Johnston
DRAWINGS BY BIRKET FOSTER: By WILLIAM FOSTER
BLACK AND WHITE DRAWING FOR REPRODUCTION:
By DONALD CAMERON-SWAN, F.R.P.S.
COMPULSORY AMERICAN PRINTING: By C.D. MEDLEY
THE ARTS & CRAFTS EXHIBITION: By B. NEWDIGATE
LITHOGRAPHY: II. THEORY: By F. ERNEST JACKSON
DECORATION & ITS USES: II. By EDWARD JOHNSTON
THE PLAIN DEALER: II. By EVERARD MEYNELL
THE COST CONFERENCE: By CECIL B. JOHNSON
AN UP-TO-DATE PLATEN: By DANIEL T. POWELL
PRINTERS' DEVICES: By the Rev. T. F. DIBDIN: PART II
NOTES AND REVIEWS. CORRESPONDENCE

Price One Shilling net

247

253

Drawings and Watercolours

Drawing and watercolour were taught at the Central School in relation to their application to design rather than as aspects of fine art.

248
Gill, Eric
Chartres Cathedral
1909. Signed and dated
Pencil and watercolour
(94 × 43)
V&A, Dept. of Prints & Drawings

249
Baker, Muriel
A Vase of Flowers
Unsigned and undated
Pencil and watercolour (366 × 231)
British Museum, Prints & Drawings Coll.

250
Doran, Joseph
Design for wallpaper, 'pomegranates, grapes and lemons'
Produced for Messrs Jeffrey and Co.
1910
gouache (92 × 52)
V&A, Dept. of Prints & Drawings

251
Davis, Louis
The Chariot of Fire
Signed with artist's monogram and dated
Easter, 1916
Watercolour (442 × 161)
British Museum, Prints & Drawings Coll.

252
Parsons, Karl
Plant drawing (Self Heal)
Pencil and watercolour
(12 × 8)
Private Coll.

253
Parsons, Karl
Portrait study
1914
Pencil (35 × 28)
Study for the head of 'Spes' (Hope) in the Rolls and Grace memorial window in Eastchurch Church, Sheppey, Kent.
Private Coll.

Artistic Crafts Series

254
The Artistic Crafts Series of Technical Handbooks
Edited by W.R.Lethaby. Published by John Hogg
'Projected as a Standard Series of Handbooks on the Artistic Crafts, suitable for Schools, Workshops, Libraries and all interested in the Arts. Each Craft is dealt with by an Expert qualified to speak with authority on Design as well as Workmanship.
All the Volumes in this Series are fully and elaborately illustrated by working Diagrams, Drawings, and Designs by the Authors and Noel Rooke – together with Collotype Reproductions and Coloured Plates.'
Private Coll.
Bookbinding, and the care of Books
By Douglas Cockerell
Silverwork and Jewellery By H.Wilson
Woodcarving: Design and Workmanship By George Jack
Stained Glass Work By C.W.Whall
Embroidery and Tapestry Weaving By Mrs Archibald H.Christie
Writing and Illuminating and Lettering By Edward Johnston
Hand-Loom Weaving: Plain and Ornamental By Luther Hooper
School Copies and Examples Selected by W.R.Lethaby and A.H.Christie. 1904
Manuscript and Inscription Letters By Edward Johnston.
With Five Plates by A.E.R.Gill. Plaster Casts of the Originals of Plates 13, 14 and 15 can be had of the Publisher.

Photographs of Central School Workshops and Student Work from the period 1896–1915

An eyewitness account of the Central School of Arts and Crafts in 1897 ('The School of Arts and Crafts' by Esther Wood, *The Architectural Review*, Vol. II, page 285)

'A sense of freshness and progress, of fruitful experiment, of new worlds yet to be conquered, pervades the whole school. In every class-room one hears the same admonition: seek to create your own style out of your own needs and materials. Take your inspiration direct from nature, and from the life of to-day. Let the materials in your hand, and the knowledge in your mind of the broad principles which the past may yield you, be but the channel through which you are to express your own personality and give your own thoughts and feelings an artistic utterance. It is the aim of each class to foster and cultivate this intelligent love of the material for its own sake, and to discover the decorative possibilities and limits of every substance handled; and the enthusiasm of every lecturer for his subject and his material is one of the most delightful features of the School.'

Lethaby's monogram

Bibliography

Books and pamphlets written and edited by Lethaby, alone or jointly

Architecture, Mysticism, and Myth
1st edition Percival 1891
2nd ed. viii + 272pp, Percival 1892
3rd ed. Introduction by Godfrey Rubens, viii + 280pp, Architectural Press 1975

Leadwork, old and ornamental and for the most part English
Macmillan 1893

The Church of Sancta Sophia, Constantinople: a study of Byzantine building; by W.R.L. and H.Swainson.
Macmillan 1894

Morris as work-master: a lecture ... at the Birmingham Municipal School of Art ... 1901.
John Hogg 1901

The Study and practice of artistic crafts:
an address ... to the Birmingham Municipal School of Art ... 1901
John Hogg 1901

London before the Conquest
Macmillan 1902

Mediaeval art from the Peace of the Church to the eve of the Renaissance, 313–1350
Duckworth 1904
2nd ed.
Duckworth 1912
3rd ed. Revised by D.Talbot Rice
Nelson 1949

The Artistic Craft Series (ed. W.R.Lethaby and Archibald H.Christie)
Vol. i School Copies and Examples 1904
Vol. ii Manuscript and Inscription Letters for Schools and Classes and for the use of craftsmen. Drawn by Johnston and A.E.R.Gill
John Hogg 1909

Westminster Abbey & the Kings' craftsmen: a study of mediaeval building.
Duckworth 1906

Form in Civilization. Collected papers on art and labour.
Oxford U.P. 1922
Reprints 1927, 1936, 1938, 1957

Simple furniture
(Reprint with corrections of 'Cabinet Making', from Plain Handicrafts, 1892.)
(Dryad Handicrafts. Dryad leaflets, No. 5 (1922))

Londinium: architecture and the crafts
Duckworth 1923

Home and Country Arts
Reprinted and enlarged from *Home and Country*, the
magazine of the National Federation of Women's
Institutes 1923

Westminster Abbey re-examined
Duckworth 1925

Medieval paintings at Westminster . . . Annual lecture
on aspects of art. 1927.
Reprinted from *Proc. of British Academy*, xiii.
Oxford U.P. (1928)

Greek buildings represented by fragments in the British
Museum
Batsford 1908

House painting and furnishing.
(Dryad Handicrafts. Dryad leaflets, No. 4 (1920))

Architecture: an introduction to the history and theory
of the art of building.
(Home University Library of Modern Knowledge.)
Williams & Norgate (1912)
Reprints 1919, 1924, 1925, 1927

Designing games
(Dryad Handicrafts. Dryad leaflets, No. 40 (1926))

Art, handicraft and education.
(Dryad Handicrafts. Dryad leaflets, No. 2 (1916))
(The place of art in education, from *Teachers' World*,
1916; Education, work and beauty, from *Parents'
Review*.)

Philip Webb and his work. (Posthumous)
Oxford U.P. 1935
Reprint with additional material
Introduction by G.Rubens
Raven Oak Press 1979

Architecture, Nature & Magic
Duckworth 1956

'Things to be Done in Architecture', a lecture delivered
to the RIBA, Jan. 24, 1917. *Journal of the Royal
Institute of British Architects* 24 (1917): 81
Reprinted in *Form in Civilization* as 'Architecture and
Modern Life'.

'What Shall We Call Beautiful? A Practical View of
Aesthetics', *Hibbert Journal*, April 1918
Reprinted in *Form in Civilization*

'Memorials of the Fallen: Service or Sacrifice?' *Hibbert
Journal*, July 1919.
Reprinted in *Form in Civilization*

'Observations and Suggestions VII–XII', *Builder* 117
(July–Dec. 1919): 11, 115, 239, 343, 463, 565

'The Royal Academy Picture Show and The Higher
Criticism of Art', *Hibbert Journal*, July 1920.
Reprinted in *Form in Civilization* as 'Exhibitionism at
the Royal Academy and Higher Criticism of Art'

'The Centre of Gravity', a lecture given at
Cambridge, England, 1920.
Reprinted in *Form in Civilization*

'Architecture as Form in Civilization', *London Mercury*
1 (1920): 574
Reprinted in *Form in Civilization*

'Greek Afternoons at the British Museum I–XII',
Builder 118 (Jan.–June 1920): (July–Dec. 1920)

'Housing and Furnishing', *Athenaeum*, 21 May, 1920
Reprinted in *Form in Civilization*

'Modernism and Design I–XII', *Builder* 120 (Jan.–June
1921): (July–Dec. 1921)

'The Architecture of Riot', *Builder* 124 (June 1923)

'The Building Art: Theories and Discussions I–XII',
Builder 124 (Jan.–June 1923): (July–Dec. 1923)

'Philip Webb and His Work I–XII', *Builder* 128 (Jan.–June 1925): (July–Dec. 1925)

'Architecture as Structural Geometry', *Builder* June 1929

'Architecture as Engineering', *Builder* 136 (Jan.–June 1929)

'The LCC New Street: Holborn to the Strand', *Architectural Review* 7 (Jan.–June 1900)

'Westminster Cathedral', *Architectural Review* 11 (Jan.–June 1902)

'The Preservation of Ancient Architecture', Address at an Architectural Conference, 1906.
Reprinted in *Form in Civilization*

'The Architecture of Adventure', Lecture given at the RIBA, London, April 18, 1910. *Journal of the Royal Institute of British Architects* 17 (1910): 469
Reprinted in *Form in Civilization*

'Design and Industry', Pamphlet entitled 'Design and Industry a proposal for the Forming of a design and industries association,' 1915
Reprinted in *Form in Civilization*

'Modern German Architecture and What We May Learn From It', Lecture delivered to the Architectural Association, January, 1915. *Architectural Association Journal* 30 (Feb. 1915)
Reprinted in *Form in Civilization*

'Political Economy or Productive Economy', A Lecture delivered to the Arts and Crafts Society, November, 1915. Reprinted in *Form in Civilization*

'The Need for Beauty', Lecture delivered to the Civic Arts Society, London, February 28, 1916
Reprinted in *Form in Civilization*

'Town Tidying', a lecture delivered to the Arts and Crafts Society, November, 1916.
Reprinted in *Form in Civilization*

'The Foundation in Labour', *Highway*, March, 1917.
Reprinted in *Form in Civilization*

A National Architecture
Whitefriars Press. Lanchester Polytechnic, Faculty of Art and Design, 1984

'The town itself: a garden city is a town'. Chap.1. (p.47) in *Town theory and practice*; by W.R.L., G.L.Pepler and others. Ed. by C.B.Purdom
Benn 1921

'Art and the Community I–III', *Builder* 138 (Jan.–June 1930)

Books on Lethaby and his time

Blomfield, Reginald
W.R.Lethaby: An impression and a Tribute.
RIBAJ 3rd ser. vol. 39 (Feb. 1932) p.293

Brandon-Jones, John
W.R.Lethaby 1857–1931. A Third Programme talk.
A.A. Journal vol. 64 March 1949
p.167 April 1949 p.194

Brandon-Jones, John
W.R.Lethaby 1857–1931
A.A.Journal vol. 64 no. 730 pp.167–171
no. 731 pp.194–196
March and April 1949

Brown, C.V.
W.R.Lethaby. Architecture as Process.
Implications for a methodology of history and criticism.
Univ. of Carolina USA
Unpublished Ph.D Thesis, 1974

Comino, Mary
Gimson and the Barnsleys. Evans, 1980

Johnston, Priscilla
Edward Johnston
Faber and Faber 1959

Johnston, Priscilla
'Lethaby and Johnston' in Lessons in Formal Writing
Lund Humphries 1984

Posener, Julius
Anfänge des Funktionalismus, von Arts and Crafts bis
Deutschen Werkbund, Berlin & Frankfurt 1964
With chapters on Lethaby, Jackson, Voysey, Ashbee,
Muthesius and the Werkbund

Macleod, Robert
Style and society: architectural ideology in Britain,
1835–1914
RIBA 1971

Martin, David S.
The Architecture of William Richard Lethaby
M.A. Thesis, University of Manchester 1957

Masse, H.J.L.
The Art-Workers' Guild
Oxford Shakespeare Head Press 1935

Mumford, L.
Foreword to Lethaby's Form in Civilization
2nd edition Oxford U.P. 1957

Powell, A.
Biographical note in Lethaby's Architecture, Nature
and Magic
Duckworth 1956

Roberts, A.R.N.
W.R.Lethaby: The life and work of W.R.Lethaby
A paper read before the Royal Society of Arts 29 March
1957
Library of RIBA
Reprinted CSAC

Rooke, N.
The work of Lethaby, Webb and Morris
RIBAJ 3rd series vol. 57 March 1950 p.167

Rooke, N.
Drawings of W.R.Lethaby
Review of exhibition RIBAJ 3rd Series vol. 39 Feb. 1932
Half a Century Old: Central School of Arts and Crafts
TLS, 28 December 1946

Rooke, Noel
Woodcuts and wood engravings: being a lecture
delivered to the Print Collectors' Club on January 20th,
1925, on the origin and character of the present school
of engraving and cutting.
Print Collectors' Club (Publication No. 5.), 1926 40p
front., illus.
Copy No. 365 of limited edition of 500 copies

Rubens, G.
'W.R.Lethaby and the revival of Printing' in Penrose
Annual 1976

Rubens, Godfrey
William Richard Lethaby: His life and work
Architectural Press 1984

Rubens, G.
Introduction to 2nd edition of Architecture, Mysticism,
and Myth
Architectural Press 1976

Rubens, G.
'Lethaby's architecture'
in Service A. (ed.) Edwardian architecture and its
Origins
Architectural Press 1975

Service, A.
Edwardian Architecture
Thames & Hudson 1977

Summerson, Sir John (ed.)
Concerning architecture
London, 1968

Thomas, Brian et al
William Richard Lethaby, 1857–1931: A Symposium in
honour of his centenary
RIBAJ 3rd ser. vol. 64 April 1957 pp.218–215

Walker, Frank A.
'William Lethaby and his "Scientific Outlook"' in
Architectural Association Quarterly, vol. 9 number 4,
1977

Ward, Basil
Preface and Epilogue to Lethaby's Architecture 3rd ed.
Oxford
Oxford U.P. 1955

Biographies of selected members of Staff at the LCC Central School of Arts and Crafts

by Michael Kennedy

J.D.Batten

b.1860, d.1932

Born in Plymouth, the son of J.W.Batten QC, John Dickson Batten intended at first to follow a legal career himself. He graduated LLB, from Trinity College, Cambridge and was called to the Bar at the Inner Temple in 1884, but soon abandoned law to study under Legros at the Slade School. Painter, illustrator and printmaker, his subject matter taken largely from mythology or fairy tales, he exhibited from 1886 at the Grosvenor, the New Gallery, the Arts and Crafts Exhibition Society exhibitions, and the Royal Academy. Elected to the Art-Workers' Guild in 1892. Taught tempera painting at the Central School from 1905 to 1909 but he is also known for his work with F.Morley Fletcher on the introduction into England of Japanese methods of wood-block printing.

S.B.Caulfield

b.1877, d.1964

Articled to J.L.Pearson RA and worked on Truro Cathedral. He set up on his own in London in 1902 after working for a firm which probably specialised in industrial architecture. Caulfield produced a number of domestic and factory buildings in the capital and its suburbs, but his greatest contribution to architecture was as a teacher rather than practitioner. Taught architecture at the Central School from 1903, at first as an assistant to Halsey Ricardo, and in 1910 was appointed Head of Department, a post he held for many years. Next to architecture the main interest in his life was cricket: he founded the Nomads cricket club in 1903 and played for them well into his later years. FRIBA, 1907.

D.B.Cockerell

b.1870, d.1945

After a short career banking in Canada, Douglas Cockerell took up bookbinding on his return to England, beginning as T.J.Cobden-Sanderson's first apprentice in 1893. Elected to the Art-Workers' Guild in 1896. He certainly taught bookbinding at the Central School from 1897 to 1904 but may have continued there as a Visitor until his retirement in 1935. Founded his own bindery in 1898 and was controller of W.H.Smith's bindery from 1904 to 1914. His work for the Ministry of Munitions, which took over Smith's bindery during the 1914–18 war, was recognised by the award of an MBE. In later years Cockerell was designated Royal Designer for Industry. He produced many bindings of rare manuscripts, chiefly for the university libraries at Oxford and Cambridge, but his best known work is probably the *Codex Sinaiticus* carried out in the inter-war years for the British Museum.

Louis Davis

b.1861, d.1941

Glass painter, book decorator and illustrator who taught drawing from the life at the Central School between 1899 and 1900. Elected to the Art-Workers' Guild in 1891. Associate of the Royal Watercolour Society, 1898.

Alexander Fisher

b.1864, d.1936

Best known as an enameller although he was also a goldsmith, sculptor and painter. Studied the techniques of enamelling in Paris and set up his own studio on returning to London in 1887. Elected to the

Art-Workers' Guild in 1894. Established his own school in Kensington in 1896. Exhibited widely and wrote for periodicals such as the *Art Journal* and *The Studio*. Taught enamelling at the Central School from 1896 to 1898.

Frank Morley Fletcher
b.1866, d.1949
Born in Lancashire and educated at University College, Liverpool. He later went to Paris where he studied at the Atelier Cormon. Taught colour wood-block printmaking at the Central School from 1899 to 1904 (he taught drawing from the life there in 1897 and 1898) and during this time he introduced into England the Japanese methods of wood-block printing. He was Head of Art at University College, Reading, from 1898 to 1906 and HM Inspector for Schools of Art from 1906 to 1908. He then became Director of Edinburgh College of Art until 1923 when he went to California to take up the post of Director of the School of Art, Community Arts Association, Santa Barbara. Elected to the Art-Workers' Guild in 1914; Fellow of British Institute of Industrial Art; naturalised US citizen, 1926. Wrote widely on art and art education. Published *Wood-block Printing* (1916) (edited by W.R.Lethaby) in an edition of 2,000, each of which contained one of his prints, the large edition made possible by his co-operative method of printing.

Arthur Eric Rowton Gill
b.1882, d.1940
Sculptor, engraver, designer and prolific writer on social, religious and artistic topics, Eric Gill was born in Brighton, the son of a nonconformist minister. He attended Chichester School of Art and then, from 1900 to 1903, was articled to W.D.Caroë in London. During this time he became interested in lettering and studied under Edward Johnston at the Central School. From 1903 he was able to earn his living as a letter cutter. He married in 1904 and, after living for a short time in London, settled with his wife and family at Ditchling in Sussex in 1907. Taught design for monumental masons

at the Central School from 1906 to 1910. Converted to Roman Catholicism in 1913 and the following year was commissioned to carve the Stations of the Cross for Westminster Cathedral. Became a lay-member of the Dominican order in July 1918 and served for a short period that year in the RAF. With Hilary Pepler and others founded at Ditchling c.1920 the Guild of St Joseph and St Dominic. From 1924 to 1928 lived near Abergavenny during which time he made wood-engravings for Robert Gibbings' Golden Cockerel Press, the Cranach Press of Count Kessler at Weimar and also designed perhaps his best known type-face, Gill Sans, for the Monotype Corporation. ARIBA, 1935: Royal Designer for Industry, 1936; ARA, 1937. Lived at Speen, Buckinghamshire from 1928.

George Jack
b.1855, d.1931
Born in New York, the son of an engraver. After his father's death he came with his mother and younger brother to Glasgow where he was educated and then articled to H.K.Bromhead. He later joined the office of Philip Webb in London. After Webb's retirement c.1900 George Jack was seen by many as his natural successor and he produced several country houses as well as some additions to Webb's work. Worked for the LCC Architects' Department. Began to carve in wood and model in clay c.1880. Designed furniture for Morris and Co., becoming their chief furniture designer c.1890. Subsequently extended his activities into designing for mosaic and stained glass. Taught wood-carving and gilding at the Central School from 1908. Member of the Art-Workers' Guild for twenty-five years and a founder member of the Arts and Crafts Exhibition Society.

F.Ernest Jackson
b.1872, d.1945
Born in Huddersfield, Jackson was a portrait painter and lithographer who trained in Paris at the Académie Julian and at the Ecole des Beaux-Arts. His reputation as an artist was obscured to some extent by a successful

Drawing of Edward Johnston
by Sir William Rothenstein, 1922

Edward Johnston at Lincoln's Inn, 1902

career in education. In addition to teaching lithography at the Central School from 1902 he also taught at the Byam Shaw School and at the Royal Academy. Member of the Art-Workers' Guild and a founder member in 1910 of the Senefelder Club, formed to encourage artists to use lithography. With Spenser Pryse he ran *The Neolith* (1907–08) a magazine in which both text and illustrations were lithographed. During the 1914–18 war Jackson was in charge of production of a series of lithographs issued by the Ministry of Information called *British Work and Ideals*, and he also designed posters for the Underground. ARA, 1944.

Edward Johnston
b.1872, d.1944
Born in Uruguay, a collateral descendant of Elizabeth Fry. On returning to England, he was educated at home owing to his poor health. In 1896 he went to Edinburgh to study medicine, but ill health forced him to abandon this. Influenced by W.R.Lethaby he began to study calligraphy and lettering, and taught writing and illumination at the Central School from 1899. Elected to the Art-Workers' Guild in 1901. He published his seminal book *Writing and Illuminating and Lettering* in 1906. Designed initial letters and headings for both the

Doves and Cranach Presses and the sans-serif alphabet for London Transport (1916–18) which is still in use. He was awarded a CBE and is generally regarded as the 'father' of the early twentieth-century revival of lettering, having influenced not only British but German designers as well.

John H. Mason
b.1875, d.1951
A compositor and self-taught classical scholar, Mason began with Ballantynes the London publishers in 1888 as a proof-reading boy. Apprenticed as compositor he stayed on as a journeyman and became the company's expert for Greek and Latin. Met Charles Ricketts through whom he was introduced to T.J.Cobden-Sanderson. Joined the Doves Press in 1900 and worked on the Doves Bible. Taught printing and typography at the Central School from 1905. Founded the journal *The Imprint* along with F.E.Jackson, Edward Johnston, and Gerald Meynell of the Westminster Press. Designed Imprint Old Face which was cut by the Lanston Monotype Corporation in 1913 and later that same year assisted Count Kessler in setting up the Cranach Press at Weimar. Royal Designer for Industry, 1938.

May Morris
b.1862, d.1938
The younger of William Morris's daughters, May (christened Mary) was born at Red House, Upton, Kent, the house designed for Morris by Philip Webb. She was educated at Notting Hill High School for Girls but studied designing from an early age and shared in her father's work, for during his lifetime she made designs for Morris and Co. and executed much of their embroidery. It was as an embroideress that she had most success and she taught embroidery at the Central School, first as Director then as Visitor, from 1899 to 1908. She made jewellery and some tapestry but also lectured and wrote on a variety of topics, most notably the life and work of her father. She served on the committees of both the Arts and Crafts Exhibition Society and the Society for the Protection of Ancient Buildings, and she was a founder member of the Women's Guild of Arts.

Karl Parsons
b.1884, d.1934
Karl Parsons began his career at 16 years of age as a pupil of Christopher Whall at the Ravenscourt Park Studio. He stayed with Whall until 1908 when he set up his own studio at the 'Glass House' in Fulham, which he kept until 1930. He began teaching at the Central School in 1904 where he took over from Christopher Whall. He worked in partnership with A.J.Overy who taught the craft processes of stained glass. His pupils included J.E.Nutgens. Parsons also taught at the Royal College for a few years before the Great War. He is known for his work in South Africa and New Zealand as well as for windows in many churches in this country. He worked closely with the architect Sir Herbert Baker.

Alfred H. Powell
b.1865, d.1960
Articled to J.D.Sedding in 1887, Alfred Powell later turned from architecture to work in a variety of crafts and is chiefly known, along with his wife Louise (née Lessore), as a decorator of pottery. He worked independently but also for a time at Wedgwood where he was responsible for introducing free-hand decoration. Taught painting on china at the Central School from 1906 to 1907. Moved soon after to Cirencester and although he had officially abandoned architectural practice he continued to produce the occasional design. Also painted in watercolour, generally landscape, architectural subjects or flowers. Exhibited widely, including the Arts and Crafts Exhibition Society and the Royal Academy.

Halsey Ricardo
b.1854, d.1928
Educated at Rugby, the son of a Bristol banker, Ricardo was an architect with private means which enabled him to accept only those commissions which he actually wanted. He always worked entirely by himself and from

Halsey Ricardo

his own home. He was articled first to John Middleton of Chelmsford and then worked for Basil Champeneys. Influenced to some extent by the work of Philip Webb. He set up on his own in 1878 and was much taken up with the decorative use of glazed tiles, giving his buildings colour and making them easy to clean. In partnership with the ceramic artist William de Morgan for ten years from 1888. Taught architecture at the Central School from 1896 to 1909. Elected to the Art-Workers' Guild in 1893 and Master in 1910.

Noel Rooke
b.1881, d.1953

Painter, engraver, book decorator and illustrator, and son of the artist T.M.Rooke who had himself worked with Morris, Burne-Jones and Ruskin, Noel Rooke was educated in France and then at the Godolphin School. He studied at the Slade School and at the Central School under Lethaby and Edward Johnston. Taught black and white illustration at the Central School from 1905, eventually becoming Head of the School of Book Production and later, Vice Principal. He was best known for his wood-engravings and was a founder member in 1919 of the Society of Wood Engravers. He was a member of both the Arts and Crafts Exhibition Society, of which he was Honorary Secretary, and the Design and Industries Assocation. His recreation was mountaineering and a number of his prints are of mountain scenes. Elected ARE, 1920.

Charles Spooner
b.1862, d.1938

Architect and furniture designer known chiefly for his ecclesiastical work. Attended classes at the Architectural Association from 1882 to 1886. Pupil of Reginald Blomfield from 1885. Taught furniture design at the Central School from 1899 assisted by his wife Minnie (née Davison) who also collaborated with him in the design of much of his church furniture and stained glass. Member of the Society for the Protection of Ancient Buildings and elected to the Art-Workers' Guild in 1887. Exhibited with the Arts and Crafts Exhibition Society and, from time to time, at the Royal Academy. Associated with Fred Rowntree in the Hampshire House workshops scheme, as were Eric Gill and Hilary Pepler. The scheme included a bakery, a publishing shop and furniture workshops, and the products of the latter were largely to Spooner's designs. FRIBA, 1907.

Luke Taylor
b.1876, d.1916

Luke Thompson Taylor was a painter and engraver who

studied at the Royal College of Art and taught etching and mezzotint at the Central School from 1908. His subject matter was largely landscape but he also engraved reproductions of contemporary paintings. Fellow of the Royal Society of Painter Etchers. Exhibited at the Royal Academy. Elected to the Art-Workers' Guild in 1907. He was killed in action in 1916 while serving with the Loyal North Lancashire Regiment.

Francis W. Troup

b.1859, d.1941

Born and educated in Scotland, Francis Troup was articled to Campbell Douglas and Sellars of Glasgow from 1877 to 1882. He then came to London and entered the office of J.J.Stephenson where he stayed for two years. He continued his architectural studies at the Royal Academy Schools from 1884 to 1886 and in 1885 received a silver medal for measured drawings. In 1888 he was awarded a silver medal in the Soane Medallion Competition. He set up his own practice at first in Bloomsbury but moved his office in 1890 to Grays Inn Square where it remained for the rest of his life. Taught lead casting and ornamental leadwork at the Central School from 1896 to 1900 during which time he was assisted by William Dodds, a registered plumber. Elected to the Art-Workers' Guild in 1895 and Master in 1923. Member of the Executive Committee of the

Society for the Protection of Ancient Buildings. His works include the meeting hall for the Art-Workers' Guild at Queen's Square (1913), the bookbinding works at Letchworth for W.H.Smith and a fine country house at Sandhills, Surrey (c.1900) but he may be better known as Supervising Architect for the rebuilding of the Bank of England. FRIBA, 1899.

Christopher Whall

b.1849, d.1924

Trained as an artist in a fairly conventional way by studying at the Royal Academy and later in Italy, but after 1879 he concentrated on stained glass and learnt his craft by working for a number of different firms. Set up on his own in a cottage in Surrey in 1884 and worked on his first important commission for J.D.Sedding. Taught stained glass and design at the Central School from 1896 to 1904 and was visiting lecturer in stained glass from 1905 to 1908. Elected to the Art-Workers' Guild in 1889 and Master in 1912. In 1890 he was a member of the sub-committee which reported to the Guild on advertisement control, and which recommended their action, but the report was turned down. He published *Stained Glass Work* (c.1900).

Henry Wilson

b.1864, d.1934

Born in Liverpool but educated at Kidderminster Art School where he followed a course in design. He was then apprenticed to an architect in Maidenhead after which he came to London and worked in a succession of offices, the last being that of J.D.Sedding with whom he collaborated on several important buildings; Holy Trinity, Sloane Street, is one example for which Wilson did much of the interior design. After 1895 he concentrated more on metalwork, jewellery, enamelling, and later sculpture, setting up his own workshop in 1898. Became first editor of the *Architectural Review*, 1896. He taught drawing from the life at the Central School from 1899 to 1908. Elected to the Art-Workers' Guild in 1892 and Master in 1917. He was President of the Arts and Crafts Exhibition Society from 1915 to 1922. Lived permanently in France after 1922.

F.W.Troup

Christopher Whall

Henry Wilson

The author of the biographies would like to
thank Mary Harper and Pat Gilmour for
their assistance.